The Jesus Way: Practicing the Ignatian Spiritual Exercises

A 19th Annotation Retreat in Daily Life

Karen R. Keen

Contemplatio Publishing
Garland, TX 75049
contemplatiopublishing.com

ISBN: 978-1-7348326-2-4

For Mom and Dad

Thank you for being the first to teach me about God.
It changed my life.

CONTENTS

Preface / 1

What are the Ignatian Spiritual Exercises? / 3

How to Make the Most of the Spiritual Exercises / 7

Principle and Foundation: Understanding God's Love and Our Created Purpose

Preparing Our Hearts for the Spiritual Exercises / 15

Week 1: Images of God / 17

What Is Your Image of God? / 19

This Is My Father's World / 21

Mothering Creator of All / 23

Who Is God in a World of Suffering? / 25

Week 2: God Created You and Loves You / 28

Week 3: Your Relationship with All of Creation / 30

Week 4: Praying for Inner Freedom / 32

Experiencing Ignatian Inner Freedom / 34

Lord, Make Me an Instrument of Your Peace / 37

Week 5: The Examen: Prayer for Discernment / 38

The Examen / 40

Emotions and the Spiritual Life / 42

Week 6: Reviewing the Journey / 46

First Week: Sin, Mercy, and Freedom

An Honest Look at What Hinders Us / 50

Praying During the Spiritual Exercises / 52

Week 7: Cosmic, Global, and Historical Dimensions of Sin / 57

    Lament: A Response to Sinful Tragedy / 59

Week 8: Remembering God's Mercy / 62

    Free Grace (And Can It Be) / 65

Week 9: Personal Sin / 67

Week 10: Sin and Mercy: Seeing the Whole Picture / 70

Week 11: Seeking Freedom, Turning from Hindrances / 72

    Come Thou Long, Expected Jesus /74

    Patient Trust / 75

Week 12: Longing for Transformation and God's Merciful Intervention /76

    O Come, O Come Emmanuel / 79

    Come Lord, and Tarry Not / 81

Week 13: Reviewing the Journey / 82

Second Week: The Life of Jesus

Coming to Know Jesus / 87

Imagination and the Spiritual Life / 89

Week 14: Anticipating the Kingdom / 92

    Contemplation of a Heroic Leader / 94

    Reading Scripture with the Senses / 97

Week 15: The Incarnation, Infancy / 99

    Incarnation Contemplation / 101

    Reflecting on Art for the Soul / 102

    O Holy Night / 103

Week 16: The Incarnation, Childhood / 105

Week 17: Two Standards: God Will vs.
Temptation / 107

Meditation on the Two Standards / 109

Week 18: Two Standards, Part 2 / 111

Week 19: Humility, Simplicity, and Inner
Freedom / 113

Three Types of People Meditation / 115

Week 20: Getting to Know Jesus / 117

Week 21: Getting to Know Jesus, Part 2 / 119

Week 22: Getting to know Jesus, Part 3 / 121

Week 23: Making a Decision in Freedom / 123

Three Kinds of Humility / 125

O God, What Offering Shall I Give? / 127

Week 24: Reviewing the Journey / 129

Third Week: Going to the Cross with Jesus

Going to the Cross with Jesus / 135

Week 25: The Walk to Jerusalem / 137

Bethany to Jerusalem Contemplation / 139

Week 26: Final Days / 140

Week 27: Arrest and Crucifixion / 142

Jesus's Arrest and Anthony Ray Hinton / 144

Week 28: Grieving Death / 146

Week 29: Reviewing the Journey / 148

Fourth Week: Resurrection and Reunion

Resurrection and Reunion / 153

Week 30: Resurrection Stories / 155

Contemplation of Jesus's Appearance to His Mother / 157

Week 31: Resurrection Stories, Part 2 / 158

Week 32: Resurrection Stories, Part 3 / 160

What Did Jesus Do with His Resurrected Body? / 162

Week 33: The Holy Spirit's Presence and Gifts / 165

Come Down, O Love Divine / 167

Week 34: Contemplation to Attain Love / 168

Fall in Love / 171

Week 35: Contemplation to Attain Love, Part 2 / 172

Take My Life and Let It Be / 174

Week 36: Reviewing the Journey / 175

Preface

I am so glad you have decided to explore the Ignatian Spiritual Exercises. This is an opportunity to have your imagination shaped by the story of "God with us." The world offers many narratives, but not all lead to life. What fills your imagination is what you become. In the Spiritual Exercises you allow Jesus to saturate your reality and invite you into true life. Ignatius of Loyola hoped that by the end of the retreat you would know God's love deeply and return God's love in such a way as to be love to others.

The Exercises are not only for personal enrichment; they are especially about shaping the way you move in the world. They are about imbibing and imitating Jesus so as to use your gifts to help others. This is why discernment and decision-making are so integral to the Exercises: active love involves making concrete choices on a daily basis.

The 9-months retreat presented here follows Ignatius's intent closely while still being readily accessible. I am indebted to those who have flavored my interpretation of the Exercises. Most significantly, Michael Ivens's commentary *Understanding the Spiritual Exercises*, trainings from Howard Gray, SJ, and a ten-months apprenticeship in the Exercises with former mentor and supervisor Michael Dante, Director of the Faber Center for Ignatian Spirituality at Marquette University. However, the retreat is my own adaptation and any inadequacies should not be attributed to them.

The retreat offers six options for prayer, contemplation, and Scripture reading per week, as well as a review day at the end of the week. Even though the retreat provides structure, there is also flexibility within that. Consider one of the following approaches and which might work best for you.

- *Taste it all.* If the Spirit has given you a deep hunger to experience all that is offered, you can complete each of the daily options. The options have been intentionally sequenced to present a train of thought or progression.

- *Take it calm and slow.* If the Spirit has given you a desire for gentle contemplation that savors small bites, you can repeat one or two of the suggested options, going deeper with them each day of the week.

- *Take it as it comes.* Perhaps you are not sure where or how to start. Maybe some weeks you have a voracious appetite and other weeks you feel the need to slow down and savor. You can let the Spirit guide as you go.

Regardless of which approach you take, keep in mind that the goal is conversation and relationship with God. Let prayer be a primary activity during your daily retreat. Talk to God about what you are feeling and thinking and listen for how God responds.

And finally, remember this retreat is not about "arriving" but about the continual process of becoming. We are always in process and will be until the end of our lives. As Paul the Apostle wrote, he pressed on toward the goal even though he had not attained it in full (Phil 3:12–14). The enemy might throw "shoulds" at you and accuse you of not measuring up, but hold fast to the truth that you are cherished by God. Our spiritual growth is fueled by love not fear.

May your heart be filled with a deep affection for God. May you know how deep and wide is God's kindness for you. May you experience the presence of Christ and radiate that presence to those around you.

Karen R. Keen, Th.M.
The Redwood Center for Spiritual Care & Education
redwoodspiritualcare.com

What are the Ignatian Spiritual Exercises?

"The Spiritual Exercises are a way of examining one's conscience
of meditating, of contemplating, of praying out loud and silently
in one's mind, and of performing other spiritual actions.
For as strolling, walking, and running are bodily exercises,
so also, in every way, we can prepare and ready the soul
to throw off all disordered tendencies that hinder us,
so as to seek and find God's will" (SE 1).

Iñigo López de Oñaz y Loyola, also known as Ignatius of
Loyola (1491–1556 AD), was a man's man, a Spanish knight
from a noble family who loved a good war and wooing
women. That is, until God captured his imagination. Ignatius
was fighting the French-backed Navarrese in the Battle of
Pamplona when he refused to retreat and was rewarded with
a shot to the legs, shattering bones. He was forced into bedrest
for several months of recovery. Bored, he asked for reading
material. The only thing available was a book on the Christian
saints and a book on the life of Jesus.

When he wasn't reading, Ignatius passed the time fantasizing.
He alternated between imagining himself as a heroic saint, like
the ones he read about, and daydreaming of being a macho
knight who wins a lady. As the days went by, he began to
notice that after daydreaming about doing the work of Jesus

he felt invigorated, the positive feelings persisted long after. But when he imagined exploits of bravado and romance, the good vibes soon dissipated, leaving him feeling discontent. From this experience he realized the power of spiritual influences and their impact on our moods, desires, emotions, and imagination. Ignatius soon committed his life to Jesus.

Ignatius lived many years in poverty, endured interrogation by Church authorities for starting his ministry without proper credentials, and went through years of schooling, all for the sake of encouraging people to follow the ways of Jesus. He lived a celibate life and devoted himself to helping others. Ignatius went on to found the Society of Jesus, also known as the Jesuits. His primary contribution was the development of the Spiritual Exercises. He designed this manual for leaders so that they might replicate his process. The Spiritual Exercises were developed out of Ignatius's own spiritual life and what he learned could help people become more fully devoted to God.

Ignatius recommended that a person go away from the world for thirty days, away from any distraction in order to pray and discern one's God-given vocation. During this time the person would be helped along by someone knowledgeable in the Exercises. However, Ignatius realized not everyone could retreat for thirty days. In his notes or "annotations" he said a person could also do the Exercises by retreating in daily life for a set period of time (he suggested 1 ½ hours a day). Since he addressed this in his 19th annotation, the Spiritual Exercises completed over several months are typically called a "19th annotation retreat."[1]

---

[1] In some circles, a "19th Annotation retreat" is treated as something distinct from the Spiritual Exercises, as though one should only call the 30 day retreat the "Spiritual Exercises." But Ignatius does not see the 19th annotation as something different from the Exercises, only an adaptation of them to meet the needs of the retreatant.

The Spiritual Exercises teach various ways of reading Scripture, praying, and discerning, all while taking a person through "Four Weeks" (originally the literal four weeks of the thirty-day retreat). The Four Weeks are built upon the Principle and Foundation of the Exercises. Today, retreatants spend time reflecting on the Principle and Foundation during preparation days prior to starting the First Week.

Principle and Foundation

The heart of the Exercises is affirmation of who we really are and our life purpose: human beings have been created to love and serve God, who is love and invites us to love. During preparation days, time is spent on the good character of God, our status as beloved created beings, and our relationship to the rest of creation. The Principle and Foundation emphasizes inner freedom to live wholeheartedly into our created purpose.

First Week

After coming to a greater understanding of God as loving creator and our life purpose as beloved creatures, we discover that certain things hinder us from loving well and, therefore, embracing our created purpose. The First Week helps us to reflect on the reality of sin and the magnitude of God's mercy in light of our faults. This Week is designed to cultivate mourning of sin, awe of God's kindness, and a hunger for freedom from all that entangles so we can embrace God's intent for our life.

Second Week

With a new hunger for freedom from sin, we more readily hear and respond to Jesus's invitation to follow him. The Second Week focuses on meditations of Jesus's life from birth to ministry days. As we get to know Jesus personally, we learn from and strive to imitate his way of life. During this time, we grow in practices of discernment and how to make concrete decisions that reflect our increasing desire to live fully for God.

Third Week

Having made a decision to respond to Jesus's invitation, we are given the opportunity to follow him all the way to the cross. The Third Week emphasizes compassion as we grow in our ability to empathize with the suffering of another. It also requires us to consider the cost of being a disciple and our own potential suffering and death, with the result that we are confirmed in our decision to follow Jesus's example.

Fourth Week

The last Week is one of joy. We spend time meditating on the many interactions Jesus had with people after the resurrection and before his ascension. We contemplate Jesus's active presence and power in our lives today. The retreat ends with the Contemplation to Attain Love where all the threads of the Exercises are brought together and contextualized in the mutual love between God and us.

How to Make the Most of the Spiritual Exercises

"It is very helpful to the one receiving the Exercises to enter into them with great courage and generosity towards one's Creator and Lord, offering to God all of one's will and liberty" (SE 5).

The Spiritual Exercises are a wonderful and unique spiritual formation experience that involve a bit more forethought and commitment than the average devotional practice. Normally, they are completed in consultation with a spiritual director who is trained to offer the Exercises and will guide you through the nine months experience. Retreatants meet regularly with the spiritual director either individually or in a small group.[2]

A spiritual director can help you discern whether this is the right season to undergo this retreat. What does this coming year look like for you? Do you have multiple obligations or transitions that might make it difficult to set aside 30–45 minutes

---

[2] If no spiritual director is available and you still want to try this retreat, be sure to find a mature Christian companion you can meet with regularly for conversation about your experience.

a day for nine months?[3] What does your current prayer practice look like? Do you sense a readiness in your heart to hear from and respond to God? These are just a few questions to consider.

Once a decision is made to proceed with this transformative experience, ponder the following recommendations to help you make the most of the Spiritual Exercises.

1. Remember you are on this journey in freedom. This is not a legalistic venture. God will not love you less if you don't do the Spiritual Exercises. You are here because some part of you really wants to be here.

2. Scope out a sacred space for your daily retreat. Decide ahead of time where you will spend your 30–45 minutes each day in prayer and meditation. This should be a quiet place where you will not be interrupted. Make this space your own (e.g. use a candle, have your journal handy, hang a picture or an icon).

3. Go at your own pace. Ignatius was very sensitive to the reality that people are at different places spiritually. There is no one-size-fits-all. He was willing to adapt the Exercises to meet the pace of the person he was walking alongside. While the goal is to complete all Four Weeks, he understood that some people might have to work up to longer periods of prayer. Or that a person might need to spend more time on one particular area or another. Even though this is a structured retreat, there is flexibility in how one incorporates various prayers or whether to spend more time on a particular Scripture than another.

---

[3] Ignatius suggested 90 minutes a day, but most 19th Annotation retreats today recognize this is a scheduling challenge for many people.

4. Document your journey. Keep a journal, doodle, paint, record your voice, collect mementos, keep a scrapbook, or any other manner of documenting your experience that suits your particular way of processing. At least weekly, capture key insights or experiences that came up for you, even if it means just jotting down a couple sentences. Sometimes it is difficult to see where you are going in the midst of it all, but when you look back at all the sign posts, it can be amazing to see what God has been revealing to you slowly over time.

5. Have essential items on hand.

- Bookmark the website ignatianspiritualexercises.com. This retreat is unique in that art and media are incorporated into the experience. Before starting the retreat view the "Supplements" page on the menu bar for instructions on how to incorporate this media.

- Obtain the book *What is Your Decision? How to Make Choices with Confidence and Clarity, An Ignatian Approach to Decision-Making* by J. Michael Sparough, SJ, Jim Manney, and Tim Hipskind, SJ. This important supplement to the retreat discusses key principles of the Spiritual Exercises as it relates to discernment and decision-making. *When you get your hands on this book, do not read it cover to cover.* Instead, read portions of it as assigned during the Exercises. Ignatius introduces certain concepts at designated times. The assigned reading dovetails with the pace suggested by him.

- Bible. The Exercises frequently engage Scripture—not as an analytical exercise, but an imaginative one.

- Journal and/or drawing paper. This is for specific activities and for recording your process. Depending on your preferences you might also use an audio recorder or other medium for documenting the journey.

- Pens/pencils, including any colored pens you might like for drawing.

6. Notice the theme and prayer for each week. At the beginning of each week, look at the theme and accompanying prayer. Each week has a particular focus and intention. Also, glance over the various options for daily retreat time. This will give you a sense of what to expect for the week, as well as guide your experience.

7. Expect meaningful times as well as boring or frustrating times. Going through the Exercises is not about achieving an ecstatic mountain top experience. It's about learning to find God in the ordinary of everyday life. It's about having greater inner freedom to live each day with more love and grace toward others. Sometimes you might be profoundly moved by a spiritual insight or the tangible presence of God. Other times you might struggle to keep your prayer time at all. Ignatius suggested that when frustration or resistance comes up to deliberately move against it. For example, when he was tempted to quit praying early or not at all, he would pray extra-long just to challenge that resistance. On the positive side, sometimes frustrations mean something is percolating that needs to percolate.

8. Don't be afraid to be honest with God or your spiritual director (and if applicable, other group members). Since you are on this journey in freedom, there is no one to impress. This is about intimacy with God that stems from full transparency and about authentic fellowship with others. You don't have to be the Super Saint. Share your joys, but share your questions and struggles too.

9. Be open to new experiences. Be open to considering new ways of praying. Be open to this process that is the Spiritual Exercises even if some of it feels unfamiliar or is different than what you might have encountered in your spiritual life or tradition thus far. A spirit of generosity toward the experience is essential.

10. Remember to keep the main thing the main thing. This is about growing closer to God and being empowered by that union to love well. Even if you can't see where it is all leading, persevere in meeting with God and let things unfold. Trust that God is at work.

THE PRINCIPLE AND FOUNDATION

Understanding God's Love and Our Created Purpose

Preparing Our Hearts for the Spiritual Exercises

We set off on our journey by first preparing our hearts for the overarching goal of the Four Weeks of the Spiritual Exercises. The Principle and Foundation of the Exercises begins with the statement that we are "created to praise, reverence, and serve God our Lord . . and the other things on the face of the earth are created for humankind that they may help him in fulfilling the end for which he is created" (*SE* 23). There are three key aspects to draw from this.

First, we recognize that we have a Creator. But before we can respond to our Creator with praise, reverence, and service, we need to know *who this God is we are being asked to love*. Is God worthy of our honor and devotion? This question prompts us to reflect on our images of God and identify misconceptions we may have (e.g. God as taskmaster). Only when we grasp the truth that God is love will our hearts truly rejoice in serving the Lord.

Second, we contemplate the reality that *we are created for a purpose*. God knit us together in our mother's womb. Our Creator wanted us to come into *being* and blessed us with meaningful work. Understanding who we really are and what we are created for inspires us to live it out.

Third, we affirm *our relationship to other created things*. As we come to marvel at the beauty of creation, we choose to interact with and steward it for God's redemptive purposes, not for exploitation or self-indulgence.

The Principle and Foundation ends with "On our part, we do not want health more than sickness, riches more than poverty, honor more than dishonor, a long life more than a short life, and so in all the rest; desiring and choosing only what most helps us toward the end for which we are created." It's not that Ignatius believed health and having our needs met are spiritual distractions, but rather the goal is acceptance of whatever God's will is even if it brings challenges.

Ignatius hoped that the Exercises would enable us to develop freedom from any inordinate attachments that might entangle and prevent us from living out our good created purpose. To help with this, the preparation days address *inner freedom* and the *examination of conscience (Examen)*. Developing inner freedom enables us to let go of things we need to let go of and live with open palms before God. The Examen is a prayer practice that cultivates spiritual discernment, especially discernment of movements within our heart that pull us toward God or away from God.

Week 1
Images of God

O God, help me to know and understand
your good and kind character.

Option 1

Reading: "What is Your Image of God?" (p. 19)

Reflection: What kind of images of God do you have? Where do these images come from? Draw each image. Ask God to help you to discern which ones are true and which are false.

Option 2

Continue to reflect and pray concerning your images of God.

Option 3

Scripture: Psalm 104

Reflection: Spend time noticing the vivid imagery in this psalm. What kind of God do you see?

Poem: "This is My Father's World" (p. 21)

Option 4

Scripture: 1 John 4:7–20.

Reflection: What is God's relationship with us? What do these verses suggest about what God's heart is like?

Option 5

Activity: Spend time outdoors in creation, contemplating what God has made. What does the art tell you about the Artist? What emotions and thoughts arise for you? Talk with God about them.

Poem: "Mothering Creator of All" (p. 23)

Option 6

Scripture: John 1:1–4, 18 and 14:7–11; Colossians 1:15–20

Reflection: Scripture says no one has seen God, but that Jesus *is* God and "explains" God. What is one positive story or impression of Jesus that comes to mind? Spend some time daydreaming about that scene. How might the person of Jesus inform an accurate image of God for you?

Reviewing the Week

Look back on the past week. What stands out to you the most as you have prayed and reflected on images of God?

Close with "My Redeemer is Faithful and True" by Steven Curtis Chapman or another favorite worship song that reminds you of God's care for you.

Note: If you have trouble this week processing a positive image of God as a result of suffering in your life or the world, see "Who Is God in a World of Suffering?" (p. 25)

What is Your Image of God?

Who is God? What do you imagine this Divine Being is like? Your image of God is likely shaped by a variety of factors, including what you were taught in your faith community, the way clergy modeled themselves, your relationship with parents, or significant life events. These can intersect with each other. For example, you might have learned to view God as a father based on Scriptures that use this metaphor. This in turn is associated with your relationship with Dad. If Dad was patient and kind this can lead to a positive image of God. But if Dad was distant or abusive, a picture of a harsh God might develop. Many of us also have impressions of God based on life circumstances. When tragedy strikes, we can easily become disillusioned. Does God not care? Why didn't God intervene?

We cannot see God physically and so we naturally draw conclusions based on what we do know: our relationships and life experiences. The biblical authors did similarly. They described God using images from real life. God is a king ruling the land (Psa 47:7–8), a humble shepherd in the field with sheep (Psa 23), an impenetrable rock (Deut 32:4), a pregnant woman writhing in labor (Isa 42:14; see also Deut 32:18), a warrior in battle (Ex 15:3), a mother hen protecting her young (Matt 23:37). God is even described as clothes you can put on (Gal 3:27).[4]

As Paul the Apostle said, we see through a glass darkly (1 Cor 13:12). Our ability to describe God in human words is limited. But this does not mean we are left only with an image of God we have invented. Just as the Israelites and early Christians encountered God, so also, we can *experience* God.

---

[4] See Lauren F. Winner's lovely discussion on this along with other metaphors for God in her book *Wearing God: Clothing, Laughter, Fire, and Other Overlooked Ways of Meeting God* (New York: HarperCollins, 2015).

How do we experience God? It may be in witnessing the beauty of a sunrise that God created. Or in the kindness of a friend reflecting Christ's love. Scripture says that the character of God is love, joy, peace, patience, kindness, generosity, faithfulness, gentleness, and self-control (Gal 5:22–23). We can recognize God's presence or absence by these traits. In fact, even though we cannot see God, we experience God in the love we give to one another: "No one has seen God, if we love one another God lives in us" (1 John 4:12). Or as Jean Valjean sings in the musical *Les Misérables*, "To love another person is to see the face of God." This is why many people have found God even in difficult times. While circumstances might not always change, it is possible to experience love or feel a supernatural peace in the middle of a storm. These spiritual experiences, along with the witness of the biblical authors help us to develop an accurate image of God.

Our image of God is significant because it affects how we understand ourselves and the way we treat other people. Who we imagine God to be is who we become. If God is hard to please, then we will naturally use others as the measuring rod for our own performance. Judging others will make us feel superior, less sinful, and therefore worthy of God's love. On the other hand, if we know the truth of God's incredible mercy toward our imperfections, we are more likely to offer the same. As Jesus said, the one who is forgiven much, loves much (Luke 7:47). Coming to experience God by noticing the fruit of the Spirit displayed in people around us and seeing God in the Person of Jesus (John 1:18), will transform our image of God, and therefore, us as image-bearers.

This is My Father's World

by Maltbie D. Babcock[5]

This is my Father's world,
And to my list'ning ears
All nature sings, and round me rings
The music of the spheres.
This is my Father's world:
I rest me in the thought
Of rocks and trees, of skies and seas—
His hand the wonders wrought.

Tis my Father's world:
The birds their carols raise,
The morning light, the lily white,
Declare their Maker's praise.
This is my Father's world:
He shines in all that's fair;
In the rustling grass I hear Him pass,
He speaks to me everywhere.

This is my Father's world:
Oh, let me ne'er forget
That though the wrong seems oft so strong,
God is the ruler yet.

---

[5] Public domain. Originally written as a poem and published in *Thoughts for Every-Day Living from the Spoken and Written Words of Maltbie Davenport Babcock* (New York: C. Scribner's Sons, 1901). It was soon put to music— the *Terra Beata* tune arranged by Franklin L. Sheppard.

This is my Father's world,
The battle is not done:
Jesus who died shall be satisfied,
And earth and Heav'n be one.

Mothering Creator of All
by Karen R. Keen[6]

I gave you birth.
A creative Mother, I bore you.
Making you in My image,
so you can steward the earth.

I sustain you.
With nurturing breasts, I feed you.
Nursing you with honey and grain,
see, how you thrive!

I comfort you.
With strong arms, I carry you.
Dandling you on My knees,
so you can play.

I guide you.
With an eagle's eye, I lead you.
Bearing you on My wings,
now you can fly too.

I call to you.
A protecting hen, I cry for you.
Gathering you under My body,
if only you let me!

---

[6] This poem draws entirely on feminine imagery of God in the Bible. See Gen 1:26–28; Deut 32:11–12, 13–14, 18; Prov 8:22–36 (God's wisdom is personified as female in Scripture; see also Prov 9:1–6); Isa 66:12–13 (see also Isa 49:14–15); Matt 23:37; Luke 15:8–10; 1 John 4:7 (see also imagery of the Spirit giving birth in John 3:5–8, and in conjunction with Gal 5:22 where love is the fruit of the Spirit). Note: The word "dandling" comes from the NRSV translation and means bouncing a child playfully on one's knees.

I look for you.
With relentless labor, I seek you.
Forgiving all, I find you.
You are My treasure.

I teach you.
With eternal wisdom, I instruct you.
Showing you how to walk,
now you know the way.

I gave you birth.
A Mother of love, I bore you.
Giving you My Spirit,
so you can love too.

Who Is God in a World of Suffering?

Exploring our images of God can sometimes trigger strong feelings of despair or anger. If God loves us and has a purpose for our lives, why is there so much suffering? What does it mean that God doesn't stop tragedy from happening? Is God truly good?

Trying to make sense of suffering is as old as Job, the biblical figure who lost everything, including his health. One common but problematic assumption is that a person did something wrong to incur God's disfavor or discipline. But, the author of the book of Job rejects claims that bad things only happen because God is angry. Often innocent people suffer. When asked why a man was born blind, Jesus denied the cause was sin (John 9:1–3). Instead he says God is actively working to bring good into painful situations. Similarly, the author of Acts describes God directly opposing the forces that cause suffering (10:38).

Anglican pastor and theologian, Rowan Williams, says when it comes to trusting God sometimes the first baby step is to look to people who "take responsibility for God." By that he means people who testify to God's goodness in hard times by their lives. When we struggle to have faith, we can lean on the faith of others.

> Faith has a lot to do with the simple fact that there are trustworthy lives to be seen, that we can see in some believing people a world we'd like to live in . . . Etty Hillesum was a young Jewish woman in her twenties when the Germans occupied Holland . . . Imprisoned in the transit camp at Westerbork . . . she wrote, 'there must be someone to live through it all and bear witness to the fact that God lived, even in these times. And why should I not

be that witness?'[7]

As you continue to process your image of God, be patient with yourself. Talk with a spiritual director, mentor, or friend who can walk alongside you. Trusting God takes time. Wrestling with pain takes time. The question "Why?" may never be answered, but it is possible to arrive at the same understanding as witnesses before us: God is light and in God there is no darkness at all (1 John 1:15).

During this time, the following suggestions may be helpful:

1. Ponder the stories of others who have suffered. For example, Nicholas Wolterstorff's *Lament for a Son*, Bryan Stevenson's *Just Mercy*, Mother Teresa's *Come Be My Light*, or Joni Eareckson Tada's *Joni: An Unforgettable Story*.

2. Engage in practices of lament. This could be as diverse as praying the Psalms, writing your own lament, or symbolic acts (e.g. tying a burden to a balloon and sending it into the sky).

3. Daydream about previous experiences of God in your life. When Mother Teresa went through long periods without sensing God's presence, her distinct and memorable call to ministry as a young woman kept her going.

4. Meditate on Scriptures that remind you of God's love, even if part of you still struggles to believe them. For example, consider contemplating stories of Jesus's caring ministry to those around him. Jesus makes God's character known in tangible ways.

---

[7] Rowan Williams, *Tokens of Trust: An Introduction to Christian Belief* (Louisville: Westminster John Knox Press, 2007), 21–22.

5. Practice self-care, including recreation/exercise, talking with trusted friends and family, eating healthy, journaling, listening to comforting music, etc.

Week 2
God Created You and Loves You

*Gracious Lord, illuminate my heart and mind to how
deep and wide is your love for me.*

Option 1

Scripture: Psalm 139:1–18

Reflection: During this week look back on your life and
consider how God has been present. Begin to create a Spiritual
Timeline starting with childhood.[8] Are there times in retrospect
that you can see God's hand in your life, perhaps in ways you
didn't notice before?

Song: "If I Flee on Morning Wings" by Fernando Ortega or
a favorite worship song that reminds you of God's presence in
your life.

Option 2

Scripture: 2 Corinthians 3:17–18; Colossians 3:9–14

Reflection: Continue to work on your Timeline. What do
you notice in today's Scripture readings about how God is
continuing to "create" you even now?

---

[8] This reflection was inspired by Andy Alexander, SJ, Maureen
McCann Waldron, Larry Gillick, SJ, *Retreat in the Real World: Finding
Intimacy with God Wherever You Are* [Chicago: Loyola Press, 2009] 1–
15).

Option 3

Scripture: 1 John 4:12

Reflection: According to 1 John, even though we cannot see God physically, we can experience God's love by the love we have for each other. Think of a time when you were loved self-sacrificially by another person. Play that scene out in your mind like a movie. How does this help you to understand how God loves you?

Option 4

Scripture: Romans 5:6–11; Luke 6:32–36; Titus 3:3–8

Reflection: Based on these readings, how far does God's love reach? Have you ever wondered whether God really loves you unconditionally flaws and all? How might these verses speak truth to replace doubts?

Option 5

Reflection: Think of one or more people for whom you have experienced a deep Christ-like love (e.g. a child, friend, person in need). Slowly play those moments back in your mind. Intentionally reflect on what it feels like to love another deeply. Then take some time to imagine God has those strong feelings of love for you. How does that affect you?

Option 6

Scripture: Romans 8:31–38 or Ephesians 3:14–21

Reflection: On a piece of paper write one or both of these passages inserting yourself as the recipient (e.g. "me" or your name). Read it out loud. What do you notice about the way God relates with you?

Reviewing the Week

Look back on the past week. What stands out to you the most as you have prayed and reflected on how God sees you? Talk with God about the different things you have noticed and felt.

Week 3
Your Relationship with All of Creation

*God help me to understand my relationship with all of creation:
other people, animals, plants, and land.*

Option 1

Activity: Draw, paint, or use clay to create scenes from
Genesis 1. As you do, honestly reflect on the ways you currently
interact with the rest of creation. Talk with God about it.

Option 2

Scripture: Genesis 9:8–17; Hosea 2:18–23; Romans 8:18–22

Reflection: Have you ever noticed that God's covenants and
redemption are not only for human beings, but also all creation?
What ideas do you have for proactively showing a similar
kindness toward other creatures and the land?

Video: Go to YouTube and watch Amazing Planet Earth
highlights to help you reflect on creation. Or search for a video
of the puffer fish's sand designs and be astounded by one of
the creatures we share this earth with.

Option 3

Scripture: Acts 17:26–28; Revelation 5:8–10 and 7:9–10

Reflection: Spend some time reflecting on the variety of
people's lives on the Humans of New York (HONY) website

(humansofnewyork.com; click on photos and read the captions). What do you notice about your connection to other human beings on this planet? Talk to God about your thoughts on the photos in light of the Scripture readings.

Option 4

Reflection: Ask God to bring to mind specific neighbors, peoples, and places. Spend some time praying on behalf of these.

Option 5

Scripture: Romans 12

Reflection: What do you learn from Romans 12 about your relationship with other people in your community and in the world? Be as specific as possible.

Option 6

Repeat or continue a reflection from one of the days this week.

Reviewing the Week

Look back on the past week. What stands out to you the most as you have prayed and reflected on your relationship with all of creation? Talk with God about the different things you have noticed and felt. Close with Psalm 148.

Week 4:
Praying for Inner Freedom

O God, help me to live with open palms and contentment, free from any misguided attachments that would distract me from your created purpose.

Option 1

Reflection: "Experiencing Ignatian Inner Freedom" (p. 34)

Option 2

Scripture: Philippians 3:7–16 and 4:4–13

Reflection: How did the Apostle Paul reach a place of inner freedom? Talk to God about where you are at in your own process and ask for greater ability to be truly free.

Option 3

Quote (from the Principle and Foundation): "On our part, we do not want health more than sickness, riches more than poverty, honor more than dishonor, a long life more than a short life, and so in all the rest; desiring and choosing only what most helps us toward the end for which we are created" (*SE* 23).

Reflection: Ignatius is *not* suggesting that we shouldn't enjoy or desire good things. But rather we should not become so attached to having something that it prevents us from doing

God's will. That includes ascetics who might want poverty more than wealth. Instead we should live with open palms, whether that calling involves wealth *or* poverty. Where are you at? What degree of inner freedom do you currently experience? *Close:* "Make Me an Instrument of Your Peace" (p. 37)

Option 4

Scripture: James 1:2–4 and 5:10–11; Psalm 88

Reflection: Growing in our capacity for inner freedom means we inevitably have to accept and lament losses. Talk with God about the Scripture readings, especially the contrast between James's understanding of joy and blessedness in suffering and the psalmist's sadness and lament. How might both approaches help you toward inner freedom?

Option 5

Repeat one of the previous days this week.

Option 6

Scripture: Mark 10:17–27

Reflection: Contemplate the struggle of the rich man to let go of his inordinate attachments. What specific things (or circumstances) are you holding onto that keep you from fully following Jesus in daily life?

Reviewing

Look back on the past week. What stands out to you the most as you have prayed and reflected on inner freedom (or "Ignatian indifference")? Talk with God about what you have noticed and felt.

Experiencing Ignatian Inner Freedom

Ignatian inner freedom refers to living life with open palms, free of inordinate attachments. When we cling to certain desired outcomes, it can prevent us from being open to whatever God wants for our lives. To have inner freedom is to relinquish demands to have our own way. Often this principle is called "Ignatian indifference." But this indifference is not to be confused with apathy or freedom from desire itself. Rather, our desires are bound up in God's desires. Ignatius of Loyola put it this way:

> On our part, we do not want health more than sickness, riches more than poverty, honor more than dishonor, a long life more than short life, and so in all the rest; desiring and choosing only what most helps us toward the end for which we are created (*SE* 23).

Ignatius certainly recognized the good of health and having enough to eat, but like Paul the Apostle, he counted it all loss for the sake of knowing Christ (Phil 3:8–10). Significantly, he not only counsels against obsessive attachments to prestige, but also attachments to asceticism. We might mistakenly believe that self-abasement earns us more love from God, or perhaps it gives us the illusion of godliness. But the issue is not whether we are living comfortably or suffering; suffering is not godlier. The point is that regardless of our circumstances, we seek to live such a life to the glory of God.

Ignatius believed that every human being's truest and deepest desire is to live out the created purpose that God has given us—namely, to love and serve God and others. We have only to become aware of that deepest desire. Inner freedom fosters that awareness. When we are in a place of open palms, we eagerly embrace and live out God's Kingdom vision, even if it involves challenges and sacrifices.

One of Ignatius's meditations illustrates different levels of inner freedom. He describes three types of people and their relationship with money. The first person wants inner freedom, but never gets around to having a serious conversation with God about her wealth. The second person also desires freedom and even takes action to use the money in godly ways. Yet instead of being truly open and asking for God's guidance, he tends to pray for God to bless decisions already made. The third person experiences true freedom. She is not attached to keeping the money, but neither is she attached to giving it away. Her only desire is to be open to whatever God would have her do with the income.

Our inordinate attachments often end up robbing us of valuable time and energy, sometimes stealing years from our lives. For example, we might cling to a relationship or vocation that is not really what God has for us, fearing loss. But often settling for second best leads to heartache or burnout. In contrast, when we live with open palms, we can live out our decisions with peace of mind and conviction, even when it requires much from us.

So how do we develop and practice inner freedom? The first place to start is getting in touch with our desires and naming them. The Examen prayer is helpful for cultivating this awareness. What emotions, desires, and thoughts are arising in you on any given day? After you recognize what you desire, you can hold it before God to discern whether that desire is leading you toward the things of God or away from God. You can also discern if you are struggling to let go of something that needs to be released.

As you examine your desires, you might find that you are being quickened by the Holy Spirit. Your desire might be an impulse from God to take action. Or if you discover an inordinate attachment that you are reluctant to let go of, you may realize an area in need of healing. Perhaps you are experiencing a subconscious anxiety or concern that is surfacing as a misguided conviction.

When we are brutally honest about strong attachments, we come face to face with ourselves and what is dictating our lives. Ultimately, our greatest joy and peace will come when we open our palms before God, entrusting the Creator with our life purpose and hope.

Lord, Make Me an Instrument of Your Peace

Lord, make me an instrument of your peace;
where there is hatred, let me sow love;
where there is injury, pardon;
where there is discord, union;
where there is doubt, faith;
where there is despair, hope;
where there is darkness, light;
and where there is sadness, joy.
O Divine Master, grant that I may
not so much seek to be consoled as to console;
to be understood, as to understand;
to be loved, as to love;
for it is in giving that we receive,
it is in pardoning that we are pardoned,
and it is in dying that we are born to Eternal Life.
Amen.[9]

---

[9] Author unknown. Commonly attributed to Francis of Assisi, this prayer likely originated in the early 1900s in France. The first known appearance in its current form was published in 1912. But, the first portion of the prayer has some similarities with a French prayer from around the 11th century. See Dr. Christian Renoux scholarship in the web post, "The Origin of the Peace Prayer of St. Francis" (http://www.franciscan-archive.org/franciscana/peace.html). See also his book *La prière pour la paix attribuée à saint François: une énigme à résoudre* (Paris: Editions franciscaines, 2001). The earliest known English translation was published anonymously in *Friends' Intelligencer* 84 (1927), 66.

Week 5
The Examen: Prayer for Discernment

Lord, please grant me greater spiritual discernment,
especially the ability to notice and respond to you each day.

Option 1

Reading: "The Examen" (p. 40)

Prayer Practice: Go through each step of the Examen, reflecting and praying over the past 24 hours. Don't worry if it feels awkward at first. You will have plenty of time to practice this way of praying in the coming months.

Option 2

Pray with the Examen by writing out or drawing your prayer. If this way of doing the Examen helps you to pray feel free to continue that approach.

Close with the "Our Father" prayer (Matthew 6:9–13)[10]

Option 3

Reading: "Emotions and the Spiritual Life" (p. 42)

Contemplate the reading and incorporate insights into today's practice of the the Examen. Notice the concepts of consolation and desolation and step 3 of the Examen.

---

[10] The Our Father is the traditional ending of the Examen that Ignatius used. However, people commonly choose to end the Examen after step 5 or use other closing prayers.

Option 4

Scripture: Galatians 5:19–23; Ephesians 4:17–24; Colossians 3:1-17

Reflection: What do these verses highlight about movements toward God or away from God?

Prayer Practice: Pray the Examen with attention to the directions you have been pulled in the last day or so. Practice noticing these movements on a daily basis.

Option 5

Activity: Tell someone today about the Examen. Explain the purpose and steps as best as you can. Consider praying the Examen together and walking this person through it. The process of talking about the Examen and practicing it with someone else will help you to better understand it.

Option 6

Prayer Practice: Pray the Examen with audio guidance from Karen. Listen as she leads you through the prayer (see the "Supplements" at ignatianspiritualexercises.com). If having audio guidance helps you to pray, feel free to continue using this approach. Also, consider making your own recording.

Reviewing the Week

Contemplate the past week. What stands out to you the most as you have prayed with the Examen? Talk with God about what you experienced in prayer this week. Continue to practice the Examen throughout your journey through the Exercises.

Additional Examen Resource:

* Mark E. Thibodeaux, *Reimagining the Ignatian Examen* (offers 34 different ways to do the Examen)

The Examen

Every day is an opportunity to be fully awake and present to the movements of the Holy Spirit. But often we are passively carried down river by all the unacknowledged thoughts and emotions that flow through us on a daily basis. We are influenced in various directions without even realizing it, distracted by a hyperactive world or numbing tasks. Staying awake requires noticing and reflecting. This is where the Examen comes in, a prayer practice developed by Ignatius of Loyola five hundred years ago.

The Examen will help you notice what is happening in and around you. It will help you to see the world through spiritual eyes. As a result, you can live more intentionally into God's purposes rather than being subconsciously tossed around by various currents. When you pay attention to your emotions, desires, and thoughts, you begin to realize how they can signal movement toward God or away from God. The goal of the spiritual life is to move closer to God and the divine will. The Examen assists us in this endeavor by illuminating when we are being pulled toward what is life-giving versus toward what is life-damaging.

The following steps of the Examen might feel awkward at first. But the more you practice this prayerful noticing, the more it will become second nature. Typically, the prayer is done once a day at a certain time that works best for you. But once it becomes part of you, the Examen is a way of life, a reflective posture and open dialogue with God throughout the day.

1. Pray for an awareness of God's presence. Remember God is with you right now. Spend 3–5 minutes in silence resting in God's presence and listening. "Cease striving and know that I am God" (Psalm 46:10).

2. Reflect on the things you are grateful for during the past 24 hours. Expressing gratitude is transformative. It changes your entire posture and spiritual outlook. Pay attention to daily subtle gifts: the unexpected smile from a stranger or friend, the beauty of trees, a task well-done, kind words, a hearty meal, or the strength to do an important but difficult thing. Spend time thanking God for these gifts.

3. Review the past day's emotions and desires. What *emotions* and *desires* are stirring? Are you feeling joyful, agitated, curious? Which ones have given you energy? Which ones have left you feeling dissatisfied or disturbed? What do these "motions of the soul" (as Ignatius called them) tell you about the directions you are being pulled spiritually—toward God or away from God?

4. Talk with God about whatever stands out to you most from your review of the day. Where do you sense the Spirit leading you? Are you being guided to pursue or resist something? Any regrets to confess? Ask God to give you the ability to see clearly and to have inner freedom to pursue what is life-giving.

5. Look ahead to tomorrow. What are you eagerly anticipating? What do you dread? Talk to God about your feelings. Ask for what you need to face and live tomorrow with love.

Emotions and the Spiritual Life

For most of his early life, Ignatius of Loyola, didn't have God on his mind. He was a man's man dreaming of war and women. But a battle wound changed his life. As he was lying in bed recovering, he noticed spiritual influences evident in the movements of his emotions and desires—or as he put it, the "motions of the soul." Bedridden and bored, he passed the time by alternating between fantasizing about acts of bravado and romantic exploits and pondering the stories of Jesus and the saints.

Ignatius began to notice that feelings of joy lasted longer after daydreaming about the ministry of Jesus. Sure, it was exciting to imagine himself as a knight seducing a woman, but the exhilaration was short-lived. He knew if he followed that path, he would miss something much more compelling: the very work of God. The emotive response to the thought of following Jesus served as a guidepost for him that led to life-changing decisions. As he paid attention to his emotions, he gained clues about whether he was being pulled toward God or away from God.

Not uncommonly people grow up in faith traditions or family systems that teach suspicion of emotions and desires. "Don't trust your feelings! They will lead you astray!" The result can be unhealthy suppression of emotions that actually makes it more likely for us to be deceived. Just as pain receptors warn us to pull our hand away from a fire, thereby protecting our body, so also our emotions and desires provide important information about our spiritual well-being. Our emotions can warn us when something is wrong or inspire us to noble heights. Ignoring our emotions puts us at risk of self-harm. In fact, scientific studies have demonstrated that suppressing emotions has a detrimental impact on health.[11]

The spiritual life is not advanced by holding all feelings in suspicion; bringing our emotions and desires into the Light allows us to *discern* what they are telling us. If we were to personify emotions, we might imagine them flagging us down, waving their arms to get our attention. Once we notice them, it's important to hold them in the light and ask, what is each emotion telling me? And is it speaking truth or a lie? How is it influencing me?

Emotions and desires are closely related to the Ignatian concepts of "consolation" and "desolation." Consolation is any movement toward what is life-giving and indicative of God's Spirit. Desolation is any movement away from God and toward destructive outcomes. *Importantly, emotions can be helpful flags for these underlying movements.* For example, warmth, patience, serenity, and love are from God. Hate, humiliation, and futility are not from God.

But we should not confuse consolation and desolation with emotions themselves. Consolation and desolation are *movements* toward God or away from God. We can feel sad and still be moving toward God, as we see with Jesus in the Garden of Gethsemane (Matt 26:37–39). Similarly, symptoms may be caused by mental illness. Such depression should not be misinterpreted as one's fault or as if one is moving away from God. Sometimes our emotions can be the result of physical conditions or brain chemistry. As you learn to discern movements of consolation and desolation, you can distinguish whether an emotion might be a flag of clinical depression or if it is related to spiritual desolation.

---

[11] A study from *Harvard School of Public Health* and the *University of Rochester* states that ignoring emotions may even increase a person's chance of premature death. Benjamin Chapman, et. al., "Emotion Suppression and Mortality Risk Over a 12 Year Follow up," *Journal of Psychosomatic Research* 75 (2013): 381–385.

Spiritual discernment is not as simple as when you happen to feel "bad" or feel "good." Noble acts of sacrifice are often difficult, while an illicit affair can feel exciting. The question is whether the *movement* is taking us toward the things of God or away from the things of God. The value of emotions is that they can help us to detect that underlying movement. As one spiritually matures and practices discernment, these subtler motions become easier to distinguish.

Consider a few examples of consolation and desolation along with possible accompanying thought patterns.

Consolation

- Joy: *This is the day the Lord has made!*
- Hope: *Even though things are hard, God will carry me through.*
- Serenity: *It is well with my soul.*
- Self-valuing: *I am fearfully and wonderfully made.*
- Conviction: *I know this is what I am meant to do, and I am willing to count the costs.*
- Self-restraint: *I want this, but I desire God's will more.*
- Inner calm and freedom: *I can let go.*
- Spirit-filled excitement: *I love the good that will come to others because of this.*

Desolation

- Futility: *Life is pointless.*
- Hopelessness: *Nothing good ever happens or ever will.*
- Restless agitation: *Something terrible is going to happen.*
- Self-loathing: *I am stupid and worthless.*
- False-guilt: *If I don't do this, I will disappoint God.*[12]

---

[12] The enemy can appear as an angel of light (2 Cor 11:4). A common way this occurs with those in ministry is to create false-guilt

- Lust: *I want this and no one is going to stop me.*
- Easy anger: *This person owes me.*
- Superficial exhilaration: *I love what this does for me regardless of how others are affected.*

Yes, some feelings can take us down a wrong path. The old adage is not completely wrong. But it is only half the truth. *Our emotions can also indicate we are on the right path.* If we are not paying attention, we might miss where the Spirit is quickening our hearts and filling us with a passion for a particular purpose. Instead of distrusting all emotions and desires, the key is to *distinguish* where certain emotions and desires originate, and how they serve as sign-posts for underlying movements of consolation and desolation. This kind of spiritual discernment can be developed as we practice paying attention, and as we learn to recognize the character and ways of God.

---

that leads to overwork and burnout. For example, a voice of desolation might say, "If you really loved God you would take this on." But that is not how the Holy Spirit speaks to us. The Spirit will inspire and empower us for the things of God.

Week 6
Reviewing the Journey

You have now gone through the Principle and Foundation, covering these themes and practices:

- Your image of God
- God's love for you
- Your relationship with other human beings and all of creation
- Inner freedom
- Discernment of spiritual influences that pull you away or toward God (consolation and desolation)
- Emotions and the spiritual life
- Examen prayer

Spend some time this week reflecting on the journey so far. Look back over your journal and other sign posts. Ask God to bring to the surface what is most important for your spiritual process. As you reflect, keep prayer at the center, not just intellectual or meditative review. The goal is always connection with God.

- What emotions come up for you as you reflect on your experience of the Exercises so far?

- What stands out to you the most? (e.g. Recurring patterns? Specific images or Scriptures?)

- Are there areas that you would like to go back to and spend more time on? If so, you can revisit them this week.

- What kind of conversations are you having with God? Are there things you have not talked with God about?

- Having completed these five weeks, draw your images of God. Are they similar or different from the ones you had when you started? How do you feel about God?

The preparation days reviewing the Principle and Foundation are designed to stir up feelings of love and desire for God. This occurs when you have an accurate image of God as a wonderful, caring Creator, and when you glimpse the meaningful life purposes God has for you. From this open-hearted disposition, you are ready to respond to what God might show you during the Exercises. Where are you at right now? Do you feel the preparation days have accomplished their purpose? Or do you need more time to reflect on your image of God and other areas? Pray and reflect on these questions. Then discuss with your spiritual director.

FIRST WEEK

Sin, Mercy, and Freedom

An Honest Look at What Hinders Us

Following the preparation days, the First Week of the Exercises begins. Once we grasp God's love for us and our meaningful created purpose, we often realize there are things that hold us back from our purpose. The 13th century monk, Gregory of Sinai wrote: "If we do not know what we are like when God makes us, we shall not realize what sin has turned us into."[13] In other words, it is only when we know our worth and destiny that we can fathom how tragic are the things that rob us. In the First Week, we are ready to take an honest look at sin and the way it hinders us. But the problem is not only our own sins; the reality includes the groaning of the whole world, longing for its redemption. As we mourn and confess sin, we become freer and able to live into God's vision for us.

The First Week can be challenging as it involves facing the reality of sin in the world, our local communities, and our own heart. That can be difficult to look at. But the goal is *not* to weigh down with hopeless guilt and despair. Michael Ivens, SJ describes the intended dynamics:

---

[13] "137 Texts: On Commandments and Doctrines, Warnings, and Promises; on Thoughts, Passions and Virtues, and also on Stillness and Prayer" in *The Philokalia, The Complete Text*, Vol. 4, comp. by St. Nikodimos, trans. G. E.H. Palmer, Philip Sherrard, Kallistos Ware (Farrar, Straus and Giroux, 1998).

Mercy, then, is the dominant theme of the First Week Meditations, but there can be no profound sense of God's mercy without a profound sense of sin. Hence the week opens up a faith-vision of sin: sin seen as the negation of praise, reverence and service, as a negative power pervading the history of free creation, as destructive of our relationship with ourselves and with the world. But sin is always considered in the Exercises in light of mercy, the mercy which is finally revealed in the Creator's commitment to sinful humanity in the cross of Jesus . . . This discovery . . . brings about a love-inspired conversion which is different from the conversion prompted by fear.[14]

If you find yourself in the next few weeks not wanting to look at sin, ask God to help you understand what is going on in your heart. Did you grow up in a harsh and condemning church environment? Does contemplating sin make you feel worthless or discouraged? Are you anxious about whether God really loves you unconditionally? Or, perhaps, you are afraid of changes that God might ask of you?

When we fully grasp God's abundant compassion toward us, we are filled with hope. Facing the reality of sin can actually inspire gratitude for God's merciful love and foster anticipation of a better world. Repentance and desire for transformation are healthy, but feelings of despair suggest possible erroneous images of God. Ask God to help you work through these deeper issues as you go through the First Week. And be sure to discuss any concerns with your spiritual director, including whether you need more time with the preparation days before moving into the First Week. It is important to have a sense of God's affirmation and good created purpose for you before looking at sin.

---

[14] Michael Ivens, *Understanding the Spiritual Exercises: Text and Commentary: a Handbook for Retreat Directors* (Herefordshire, UK: Gracewing, 1998), 44.

Praying During the Spiritual Exercises

One of the gifts of the Spiritual Exercises is the opportunity to explore various ways of praying. You have already been introduced to the Examen, which Ignatius considered to be primary and essential to the Exercises. As you learn about these prayers, continue practicing them throughout the coming months of the retreat. Over time you may gravitate toward some forms more than others or find ways to adapt them that best work for you. Consider not only the method of the prayers, but especially the intention behind why Ignatius suggested it. You don't need to try to force every single prayer type you learn into each day's retreat time. *Go with how the Spirit is leading you to pray.* The most important thing is meaningful conversation with God through daily prayer.

As you go into the First Week, the prayer forms described below will be introduced. You will be prompted to try one at specific times, so don't worry about trying them all at once. When you are prompted, simply flip back to this page to revisit the instructions. Remember that anything new can feel awkward at first, so give it time. Once you have been introduced to a prayer form, you can use it anytime you want during the Exercises without any prompting.

Traditional Prayers

Sometimes when we don't have our own words, praying with fellow pilgrims from throughout the ages can help us know what to say or ask of God. *Anima Christi* is a traditional prayer that dates to about the 14th century AD.[15] Ignatius frequently referred to it. The *Our Father* is also a traditional prayer that comes directly from Scripture.

---

[15] The author is unknown.

Anima Christi (Soul of Christ)

Soul of Christ, sanctify me.
Body of Christ, rescue me.
Blood of Christ, overwhelm me.
Water from the side of Christ, wash me.
Endurance of Christ, strengthen me.[16]
O good Jesus, hear me.
In your wounds hide me.
Do not let me be separated from you.
From the evil one, protect me.
In the hour of my death call me,
and bid me come to you,
that with your saints I may praise you
forever and ever. Amen.

Our Father

Our Father in heaven, hallowed be your name. Your kingdom come. Your will be done, on earth as it is in heaven. Give us this day our daily bread. And forgive us our debts, as we also have forgiven our debtors. And do not bring us to the time of trial, but rescue us from the evil one (Matt 6:9–13).

Use of the Body in Prayer

Ignatius believed that being fully engaged in the spiritual life meant using not only our mind, but also our body and senses. To facilitate a heartfelt response to God, he wanted us to bring our whole selves. This is similar to what we see in the

---

[16] The word translated "endurance" is the Latin term *passio* or Passion of Christ, which refers to Jesus's suffering on the cross and what it accomplished. But the word also has the connotation of endurance. Namely, the strength of Jesus to persevere amid his suffering.

Psalms when the biblical authors describe raising one's hands, kneeling, walking in procession, or other bodily movements in prayer (e.g. Psalm 34:2; 42:4; Lam 2:10). One practice Ignatius suggested was to enact in some way a day's retreat focus. For example, for the days that address sin, he suggested acts of mourning and repentance. You could wear all black, close the curtains or blinds and turn off the lights, clutch your hand across your chest, or even put dust on your head. The specific type of act is less important than a heartfelt demonstration. You can be creative in how you might bring your body and senses into the intentions of the retreat time.

Praying and Reading Scripture with the Senses

Often during the Exercises, you might be asked to read a Scripture passage and enter the story with your senses. What do you see, taste, touch, smell, hear? The goal is to make the biblical narrative come alive. Ignatius did not want us to succumb to emotionally detached Scripture reading and prayer, but to go back in time as if Jesus was standing right in front of us. Entering the story with your senses, allows you to hear Jesus talking, feel the dust on your feet, and smell the bustling crowd.

- What details do you notice when using your senses?
- Where do you find yourself in the story?
- What emotions or reactions arise for you?
- What insights surface about God, yourself, and the Christian life?

As you read, talk with God about what you are experiencing. In fact, you can talk with Jesus as if you were there in that 1st century moment. What might you say or ask? Is it different or the same as what the other people in the scene are saying?

Preparatory Prayer

One format of prayer that Ignatius introduced is designed to prepare your heart for going into each day's retreat time. It is a warm-up, so to speak. Ignatius wanted us to engage authentically with the Exercises and not fall into mechanical, detached prayer. When we have had a busy day and our mind is on a million other things, the preparatory prayer helps us to become centered and fully present for our retreat with God. Think of it as pausing for a moment before you jump into that day's devotional time. It has three aspects:

Step 1: Opening Prayer:

Lord, please give me grace so that all my intentions and actions are focused solely on honoring and serving you. (Always the same. Feel free to put the intention of this prayer in your own words).

Step 2: Readying the Heart

Take a moment to ready your heart for that day's Scripture reading and reflection. Do this by considering the subject you are about to focus on and bringing your heart into a congruent disposition. For example, if the subject is resurrection, ready your heart for joy. If the subject is sin, seek a posture of mourning and humility.

Step 3: Request

For the purposes of this particular retreat, each week has a prayer of request written at the top of the page. So, for the week on global and historical dimensions of sin, the prayer request is: "Savior of all, give me a clear awareness and sensitivity to the magnitude and severity of sin, as well as a heartfelt ability to mourn it."

Triple Colloquies

The Triple Colloquies (or three conversations) is a repetition of prayer asking the three persons of the Trinity for help in becoming free from all that entangles.[17] The prayer includes the *Anima Christi* and the *Our Father*. A colloquy is a conversation, so feel free to put these thoughts in your own words. At the end, pause to listen for God's response:

Holy Spirit, please open my eyes so I can recognize sin clearly. Give me the ability to see and feel the harm caused by it. Fill me with a willingness to change anything that needs to change. Increase my discernment so that I experience a deep aversion to ungodliness and a desire to abandon such things.

Jesus, please open my eyes so I can recognize sin clearly. Give me the ability to see and feel the harm caused by it. Fill me with a willingness to change anything that needs to change. Increase my discernment so that I experience a deep aversion to ungodliness and a desire to abandon such things.

Pray the Anima Christi (p. 53)

Father, please open my eyes so I can recognize sin clearly. Give me the ability to see and feel the harm caused by it. Fill me with a willingness to change anything that needs to change. Increase my discernment so that I experience a deep aversion to ungodliness and a desire to abandon such things.

Close with the Our Father (Matthew 6:9–13; p.53)

---

[17] Ignatius sometimes says to ask Mary to pray on one's behalf, along with praying to the Son and Father. At other times he suggests praying to the Trinity. To make this retreat accessible to both Catholics and Protestants, I have placed emphasis on the Trinitarian prayer. This is in keeping with Ignatius's belief that each person of the Godhead is involved in our spiritual formation.

Week 7

Cosmic, Global, and Historical Dimensions of Sin

Savior of all, give me an awareness and sensitivity to the magnitude and severity of sin, as well as a heartfelt ability to mourn it.

Option 1

Preparatory Prayer (p. 55; try starting with this throughout the week and on-going)

Scripture: Jude 1:6; 1 Peter 5:8–9

Quote: According to Christian tradition, certain angels fell into sin before human beings did. Ignatius writes: "Bring to memory the sin of the angels, how they, being created in grace, did not help themselves by using their freedom to reverence and obey their Creator and Lord; but becoming prideful, they were changed from grace to malice, and hurled from Heaven to Hell" (*SE* 50).

Reflection: Contemplate the beginning of time when sin preceded even humankind, and how this cosmic dimension of evil power still exists.

Option 2

Scripture: Genesis 2–3

Reflection: Consider how sin has been present among the human race long before you were born. Visualize the events in Genesis 2 and 3 (see page 54 for more on reading and praying Scripture with the senses).

Option 3

Reflection: Look at recent news headlines. What troubles stemming from sin in the world especially grieve your heart? Contrast this with what you learned about our created purpose during reflection on the Principle and Foundation. Spend time interceding in prayer for specific people and circumstances that come to your mind.

Option 4

Reading: "Lament: A Response to Sinful Tragedy" (pg. 58)

Reflection: Spend some time contemplating lament. What practices of lament did you grow up with, if any? Does your Christian or cultural tradition offer any resources of lament? What practices of lament might you incorporate into your life in response to sinful tragedy?

Option 5

Scripture: Psalm 10 and/or Psalm 31

Activity: Write your own psalm of lament regarding suffering caused by sin that you have witnessed in your community recently.

Option 6

Scripture: Romans 3:9–20

Reflection: What comes up for you as you read these verses, especially in light of previous days' reflections? What do you feel? Talk with God about it.

Reviewing the Week

Look back on the past week. What stands out to you the most as you have prayed and reflected on the real power of sin in the world? Talk with God about your reflections.

Lament: A Response to Sinful Tragedy

In an age of constant video streams, images, and graphic accounts of turmoil around the world and in our communities, we can become emotionally paralyzed. The trauma caused by sinful humanity is overwhelming, leaving us unequipped to handle the feelings that arise. Sometimes we shut off and numb ourselves to it all. The danger is that we disengage and no longer actively pursue change. Most of us don't want to lose the ability to empathize. Yet, how do we remain sensitive to the gravity of sin without losing our minds?

That question has more than one answer, but the biblical authors set an example for us. They were well-acquainted with tragedy, and their response was to lament. Lament gives us space to process and express the pain sin causes. In the book of Lamentations, we hear the cry of distress. It comes from the pen of an ancient Jewish author who captured the immense pain of war and exile.[18]

How lonely sits the city
that once was full of people!
How like a widow she has become,
she that was great among the nations!
She that was a princess among the provinces
has become a vassal . . .
Judah has gone into exile with suffering
and hard servitude;
she lives now among the nations,

---

[18] This anguish was compounded by the belief that God was punishing them for sin—a common belief in the ancient Near East to explain why bad things happen. It was a theological form of victim blaming. But not all the biblical authors believed defeat in war or other calamities were the result of God's punishment. The authors of Ecclesiastes and Job both concluded that the cause of suffering is a mystery and that even good people can experience tragedy.

and finds no resting place;
her pursuers have all overtaken her
in the midst of her distress (Lam 1:1, 3)

My eyes are spent with weeping;
my stomach churns;
my bile is poured out on the ground
because of the destruction of my people,
because infants and babes faint
in the streets of the city.
They cry to their mothers,
"Where is bread and wine?"
as they faint like the wounded
in the streets of the city,
as their life is poured out
on their mothers' bosom (Lam 2:11–12).

Yohanna Katanacho, a Palestinian theologian, knows tragedy and lament. He has seen the terrible violence both Israelis and Palestinians have inflicted on each other. In an interview with BMS World Mission he stated:[19]

The Book of Lamentations talks about a situation very similar to what is happening in Gaza. I'm trying to seek God through my tears, seek my humanity through my tears as well as the tears of others. We as human beings are unique, we can cry, we can feel our pain but our humanity becomes even deeper and stronger when we start to feel the pain of other people around us . . . Many times, when we start arguments of who's right and who's wrong, it becomes so difficult and we don't get to solutions.

---

[19] "A Poem of Lament for Both Sides of Gaza," BMS World Mission website, 17 July 2014, http://www.bmsworldmission.org/news-blogs/archive/a-poem-lament-both-sides-gaza. See also his poem in this article.

But perhaps instead of starting our interactions with arguments and reading different newspapers, perhaps we can just cry with people who are suffering and not just cry with our friends but also with our enemies.

Lament, paradoxically, is a sign of hope, an indicator that the one crying out still believes Someone is listening. Where there is no hope, there is no wailing—only silent resignation.[20] Lament is a way to express all that we feel inside when tragedy consumes us—despair, fear, anger. But lament is not only the expression of pain; it's also the demand for change. It is a protest against what is happening and an expectation that God can and must respond. Even in the face of death, lament pleads for the long-awaited resurrection.

Lament can be done individually or communally with others. In community, we hold each other's pain. We are not alone; together we find strength. This might look like a candle light vigil. Or it might look like a literal protest, marching in the streets, making the world know and hear our suffering. Lament is not only for the ears of God, but for each other. We are meant to hear each other's pain, to empathize, and to rebuild together.

Many of us in the West never learned how to lament. It is a long-lost practice. We did not learn the rituals of wailing, or tearing our clothes, or putting dust on our heads, or writing our anguish in poetry, or wearing black for a season. We are expected to put on a strong face, bottle our emotions, and return to the office, pretending that nothing has happened. But the power of lament is that it disrupts the routine. It says, "No, everything is not all right." That honesty is a call for empathy and solidarity. And it's a cry against the ravages of sin, saying "The world can be a better place. Let's, you and I, work together to make it so."

---

[20] Dr. Ellen F. Davis, Duke Divinity School lecture.

Week 8
Remembering God's Mercy

*Compassionate God, help me to grasp how incredibly deep
and endless is your mercy toward us all.*

Option 1

Scripture: John 1:1–18

Reflection: Having spent time last week reflecting on the
devastating impact of sin, consider anew how God chose to
respond to our turmoil. Where do you see God's light showing
up in your life and community?

Option 2

Scripture: Romans 5:6–11; Ephesians 2:4–9

Song: "And Can It Be That I Should Gain?" (p. 65)

Reflection: Ignatius encourages us to have a conversation
with God, asking the following two questions (*SE* 53). They are
in response to the awe of God's mercy toward us. Imagine
Jesus on the cross as you do this reflection.

1. "How can it be that God, the Creator, became a human
being, and from eternity came to temporal death, and so to
die for my sins?"

2. "What have I done for Christ, what am I doing for Christ, what ought I to do for Christ?"

Option 3

Scripture: Romans 8:31–39

Activity: Write, draw, or have a conversation with a friend about the most significant experiences of mercy and forgiveness that a) you have witnessed and b) you have personally received. What feelings arise knowing this is what God's mercy is like for you? Talk with God about your reflections.

Option 4

Reflection: Spend some time soaking in the details of "Woman Caught in Adultery"—a painting by Woonbo Kim Ki-chang. How does this painting help you to internalize God's merciful response to sin?

Option 5

Scripture: John 11:1–44

Reflection: As you read the Lazarus story, consider how the burial clothes wrapped around him represent sin. Contemplate how God weeps over our death and in compassion calls us forth from the grave to give us life and healing.

Song: "Broken Things" by Julie Miller (as sung by Mindy Boyd; see "Supplements" on website).

Option 6:

Scripture: Philippians 2:5–11.

Reflection: Continue to prayerfully reflect on these two questions in light of God's mercy (see Option 2):

1. "How can it be that God, the Creator, became a human being, and from eternity came to temporal death, and so to die for my sins?"

2. "What have I done for Christ, what am I doing for Christ, what ought I to do for Christ?"

Reviewing the Week

Look back on the past week. What stands out to you the most as you have prayed and reflected on God's mercy? Talk with God about your reflections. Close with the Our Father.

Free Grace
(And Can It Be?)
by Charles Wesley[21]

And can it be, that I should gain
An int'rest in the Saviour's blood!
Dy'd he for me? —Who caus'd his pain!
For me? —Who him to death pursu'd.
Amazing love! How can it be
That thou, my God, shouldst die for me?

'Tis myst'ry all! Th' immortal dies!
Who can explore his strange design?
In vain the first-born seraph tries
To sound the depths of love divine.
'Tis mercy all! Let earth adore;
Let angel minds enquire no more.

He left his Father's throne above,
(So free, so infinite his grace!)
Empty'd himself of all but love,
And bled for Adam's helpless race:
'Tis mercy all, immense and free!
For O my God! It found out me!

Long my imprison'd spirit lay,
Fast bound in sin and nature's night:
Thine eye diffus'd a quick'ning ray;
I woke; the dungeon flam'd with light;
My chains fell off, my heart was free,

---

[21] Charles Wesley, "Free Grace" in *Hymns and Sacred Poems* (London: Strahan, 1739), 117–119. Originally entitled "Free Grace," this hymn is popularly known as "And Can It Be That I Should Gain" set to music by Thomas Campbell.

I rose, went forth, and follow'd thee.
Still the small inward voice I hear,
That whispers all my sins forgiv'n;
the atoning blood is near,
That quench'd the wrath of hostile heav'n:
I feel the life his wounds impart;
I feel my Saviour in my heart.

No condemnation now I dread,
Jesus, and all in him, is mine:
Alive in him, my living head,
And cloath'd in righteousness divine,
Bold I approach th' eternal throne,
And claim the crown, thro' Christ, my own.

Week 9

Personal Sin

*Gracious God, please soften my heart so that I can truly grieve
and repent the sins of my past and present.*

Option 1

Scripture: 1 John 1:5–2:2

Reflection: Consider your past sins. Ignatius suggests calling
to mind places you have lived, people you have known, and
particular occupations in order to facilitate the reflection. The
goal here is not to laden with guilt, but to own the truth that
each of us has and does participate in sin. Transformation
begins with honesty. And transformation is possible because
God readily forgives and desires to help us love better. Close
with Psalm 130.

Option 2

Scripture: James 5:16; John 3:20–21

Listen: On Being podcast, "The Refreshing Practice of
Repentance" by Jewish thinker Louis Newman.

Activity: Sin is often fueled by secrecy and fear of admitting
imperfections. Confession is good for the soul. Begin a new
regular spiritual practice of repentance and confession to
trusted pastors and friends. What might you start with this
week?

Close with *Anima Christi* (p. 53)

Option 3

Scripture: Meditate on and pray with Psalm 51.

Reflection: Consider various sins you struggled with this week. What fosters them? Lament and confess your sins to God, knowing God is faithful to forgive them.

Activity: Try bringing your body into prayerful confession (see pages 53–54 for praying with the body).

Option 4

Scripture: Matthew 5:21–24

Reflection and activity: Ask God to bring to mind a specific person(s) with whom you need to make amends or reconcile. Write a letter. Make a phone call. Meet them in person. Ask God to give you courage, wisdom, and humility.

Option 5

Scripture: Luke 18:9–14

Reflection: Enter the scene. Where do you find yourself in this story? (see p. 54 for how to experience the story with all your senses)

Close with the Triple Colloquies (p. 56)

Option 6

Reread: "The Examen" (p. 40)

Reflection: Look back on the past day using the Examen and consider where you would have liked to have done things differently. Ask God to give you insight into what contributes to certain sinful thoughts, attitudes, and behaviors. Ask God to empower you with the Holy Spirit to overcome these.

Reviewing the Week

Look back on the past week. What kind of emotions and thoughts have come up for you? Ignatius hoped that by reflecting on sin and mercy that we would 1) be awakened to areas where we are not living out our created purpose and mourn that tragic reality and 2) be awakened to God's amazing mercy that helps us return to loving well. Have the reflections accomplished this goal? Why or why not? Talk with God honestly about where you are at.

Week 10
Sin and Mercy: Seeing the Whole Picture

*Merciful One, give me a deep heart knowledge of your mercy
and confidence in your unconditional love.*

Option 1

Reflection: When the First Week was introduced in this
book, it was mentioned that looking at sin might trigger certain
reactions. Have any of those issues come up for you? How do
your responses shed light on your current image of God? View
the chart "Legalism, Licentiousness, or Christianity?" (see
"Supplements"). Where do you find yourself? Talk with God
about your reflections.

Option 2

Scripture: Luke 15:11–32

Reflection: "Reconciliation" sculpture by Margaret Adams
Parker based on Luke 15 (see "Supplements"). If you didn't
know the biblical story already, who might be mistaken as
representing God in this sculpture? How might this sculpture
helpfully shape your image of God's response to sin?

Close with *Anima Christi* (p. 53).

Option 3

Scripture: Repeat Luke 18:9–14

Prayer Practice: Triple Colloquies (p. 56)

Song: "Wonderful, Merciful Savior" sung by Susan Ashton

Option 4

Scripture: Luke 6:35–36; Titus 3:3–8

Activity: We come to understand God's mercy better by giving and receiving it from one another. Engage in an act of mercy this week. Think of someone you know who has recently made a mistake that troubles you or has done something to offend you. Spend time praying for this person. Ask God to give you concrete ideas of how to show mercy to this person.

Option 5

Scripture: Luke 7:36–50

Reflection: Enter the scene with your senses. How does Jesus respond to the woman in this passage? How does knowing God's mercy change you?

Option 6

Repeat any of the days this week.

Reviewing the Week

Look back on the past week. What stands out to you the most as you have prayed and reflected on the reality of sin and God's merciful response? Talk with God about your reflections.

Week 11
Seeking Freedom,
Turning from Hindrances

*O God, increase my hunger to follow Christ wholeheartedly
and set me free from all that hinders.*

Option 1

Scripture: Philippians 3:1–14

Re-Read: "Experiencing Ignatian Inner Freedom" (p. 34)

Reflection: As you anticipate God's Advent (arrival), identify any remaining obstacles to following God wholeheartedly. Are there ways you are still holding back? What is your level of inner freedom? Talk with God about this.

Activity: How might you express or enact in a physical way your longing for freedom? Be creative as the Spirit leads.

Option 2

Scripture: Repeat Philippians 3:1–14

Option 3

Reading: "Making Sense of Inner Spiritual Movements" in the assigned book *What's Your Decision?* [22]

Prayer: If you haven't prayed with the Examen for a while,

---

[22] Chapter 5 in the book J. Michael Sparough, et. al, *What's Your Decision? How to Make Choices with Confidence and Clarity: An Ignatian Approach to Decision Making* (Chicago: Loyola Press, 2010).

renew that practice today, paying attention to those inner movements.

Option 4

Scripture: Galatians 5:13–26

Reflection: Becoming free requires discernment. Pray the Examen with the purpose of growing in the ability to perceive on a daily basis the things that are of the Spirit and the things that are not.

Song: Contemplate and sing the words of the Advent song "Come Thou Long Expected Jesus" as a prayer to close (p. 74).

Option 5

Scripture: 1 John 4:1–6; Ephesians 2:1–2 and 6:10–18

Reflection: Reflect on these verses and the reality of spiritual influences. What are your thoughts? Talk with God about them.

Close with the Examen prayer.

Option 6

Scripture: Repeat Galatians 5:13–26

Prayer Practice: Pray the Examen

Close: "Patient Trust" by Pierre Teilhard de Chardin (p. 75)

Reviewing the Week

Look back on the past week. What stands out to you the most as you have prayed and reflected on longing for freedom from all that entangles? Talk with God about your reflections.

Come Thou Long, Expected Jesus
by Charles Wesley[23]

Come, Thou long-expected Jesus,
Born to set Thy people free;
From our fears and sins release us,
Let us find our rest in Thee.
Israel's strength and consolation,
Hope of all the earth Thou art;
Dear desire of every nation,
Joy of every longing heart.

Born Thy people to deliver,
Born a child and yet a King,
Born to reign in us forever,
Now Thy gracious kingdom bring.
By Thine own eternal Spirit
Rule in all our hearts alone;
By Thine all-sufficient merit,
Raise us to Thy glorious throne.

---

[23] Charles Wesley, "Hymn X," *Hymns for the Nativity of our Lord* (London: Strahan: 1745).

Patient Trust
by Pierre Teilhard de Chardin[24]

Above all, trust in the slow work of God.
We are quite naturally impatient in everything to
reach the end without delay.
We should like to skip the intermediate stages.
We are impatient of being on the way
to something unknown, something new.
And yet it is the law of all progress
that it is made by passing through
some stages of instability—
and that it may take a very long time.
And so, I think it is with you;
your ideas mature gradually—let them grow,
let them shape themselves, without undue haste.
Don't try to force them on,
as though you could be today what time
(that is to say, grace and circumstances
acting on your own good will)
will make of you tomorrow.
Only God could say what this new spirit
gradually forming within you will be.
Give Our Lord the benefit of believing
that his hand is leading you,
and accept the anxiety of feeling yourself
in suspense and incomplete.

---

[24] The author (1881–1955) was a Jesuit. It's unclear when this reflection first became publicly available. He may have written it in a letter to his niece and from there became popularly distributed.

Week 12
Longing for Transformation and God's Merciful Intervention

Lord, fill me with a longing to see myself and the world transformed. Have mercy and intervene amid our weaknesses.

Option 1

Reading: "O Come, O Come Emmanuel" (p. 79)

Reflection: Sometimes we have heard Advent songs so often we no longer truly *hear* the words.[25] Meditate on this song in light of the past several weeks. What words, phrases, or images stand out to you the most? Why might that be? Talk with God about your reflections.

Close by singing the song as your prayer.

Option 2

Reflection: What redemption are you longing for in your own life? What redemption do you desire to see in your community? How is your heart doing in the waiting for it? Henri Nouwen once wrote:

How do we wait for God? We wait with patience. But patience does not mean passivity. Waiting patiently is not

---

[25] Note: Advent songs long for and anticipate Christ's arrival. Christmas songs celebrate the fact that Christ has finally come.

like waiting for the bus to come, the rain to stop, or the sun to rise. It is an active waiting in which we live the present moment to the full in order to find there the signs of the One we are waiting for.[26]

Nouwen goes on to say that waiting is a kind of suffering that effects something in us, causing us to grow strong over time. He says waiting means being alert to the here and now so that we don't miss the first signs of God's coming.

As you ponder Nouwen's understanding of waiting, talk with God about it.

Option 3

Scripture: Isaiah 61; Luke 4:14–28

Reflection: How do these Scriptures reveal God's mercy in history and now? Enter the scene. Imagine being in the audience hearing the prophet Isaiah or Jesus read these words aloud. How do you respond?

Option 4

Reading: "Come Lord and Tarry Not" (p. 81).

Reflection: Ponder this Advent song. What words, phrases, or images stand out to you the most? Talk with God about what you notice.

Option 5

Repeat one of the previous days this week.

Option 6

Reflection: Sometimes, while waiting for God to intervene, we can begin to doubt God's power or willingness to show up. When the Israelites felt this way, they recalled God's past

---

[26] Henri J. M. Nouwen, *Bread for the Journey: A Daybook of Wisdom and Faith* (New York: HarperOne, 2006), 20.

actions. Return to your Spiritual Timeline (p. 17). Spend some time meditating on where you have seen God act in your life in the past. Even consider how God has worked in your heart since you started the Spiritual Exercises.

Reviewing the Week

Look back on the past week. What stands out to you the most as you have prayed and reflected on longing for transformation and God's merciful intervention? Talk with God about your reflections. Close with your favorite Advent song.

O Come, O Come Emmanuel
Translated by John Mason Neale[27]

O come, O come, Emmanuel,
And ransom captive Israel,
That mourns in lonely exile here,
Until the Son of God appear.
Rejoice! Rejoice! Emmanuel
Shall come to thee, O Israel.

O come, Thou Rod of Jesse, free
Thine own from Satan's tyranny;
From depths of hell Thy people save,
And give them victory o'er the grave.
Rejoice! Rejoice! Emmanuel
Shall come to thee, O Israel.

O come, Thou Dayspring, from on high,
And cheer us by Thy drawing nigh;
Disperse the gloomy clouds of night,
And death's dark shadows put to flight.
Rejoice! Rejoice! Emmanuel
Shall come to thee, O Israel.

O come, Thou Key of David, come
And open wide our heav'nly home;
Make safe the way that leads on high,
And close the path to misery.
Rejoice! Rejoice! Emmanuel
Shall come to thee, O Israel.

---

[27] William Henry Monk, ed., "The Redeemer Shall Come to Zion" in *Hymns, Ancient and Modern with Accompanying Tunes*, Trans. John Mason Neale (New York: Port, Young, and Co., 1876), 31. This song is taken from the O Antiphons of the Middle Ages, originally in Latin.

O come, Adonai, Lord of might,
Who to Thy tribes, on Sinai's height,
In ancient times didst give the law
In cloud and majesty and awe.
Rejoice! Rejoice! Emmanuel
Shall come to thee, O Israel.

Come Lord and Tarry Not
Words by Horatius Bonar[28]

Come, Lord, and tarry not;
Bring the long-looked-for day!
O why these years of waiting here,
These ages of decay?

Come, for Thy saints still wait;
Daily ascends their sigh;
The Spirit and the Bride say, "Come";
Does Thou not hear the cry?

Come, for creation groans,
Impatient of Thy stay,
Worn out with these long years of ill,
These ages of delay.

Come, for love waxes cold,
Its steps are faint and slow;
Faith now is lost in unbelief,
Hope's lamp burns dim and low.

Come in Thy glorious might,
Come with the iron rod,
Scattering Thy foes before Thy face,
Most mighty Son of God!

Come, and make all things new,
Build up this ruined earth;
Restore our faded Paradise,
Creation's second birth.

---

[28] Horatius Bonar, *Hymns of Faith and Hope* (London: James Nisbet, 1857). Stanzas 1–3, 11, 13.

Week 13
Reviewing the Journey

You have now gone through both the Principle and Foundation of the Exercises and the First Week, covering these themes:

From Principle and Foundation
- Your image of God
- God's love for you
- Your relationship with other human beings and all creation
- Inner freedom
- Discernment of spiritual influences that pull us away or toward God (consolation and desolation)
- Emotions and the spiritual life

From First Week
- Cosmic, global, and historical dimensions of sin
- Personal sin
- God's mercy
- Inner freedom and spiritual discernment (continued)
- Longing and praying for transformation (global and personal)

You have also been introduced to different types of prayer:
- Examen
- Traditional prayers (e.g. *Anima Christi*)

- Preparatory prayer
- Praying with the body
- Praying Scripture with the senses
- Triple Colloquies

Spend some time this week reflecting on the journey so far. Look back over your journal and other sign posts. Ask God to bring to the surface what is most important for your spiritual process. As you reflect, keep prayer at the center, and not just intellectual or meditative review. The goal is always connection with God.

- What emotions or desires come up for you as you reflect on your experience of the Exercises so far, especially the First Week?

- What stands out to you the most? (e.g. Recurring patterns? Specific images or Scriptures?)

- Are there areas that you would like to go back to and spend more time on? If so, you can revisit them this week.

- What kind of conversations are you having with God? Are there things you have not talked with God about?

- How are you doing with practicing discerning, on a daily basis, spiritual movement toward God or away from God? What movements have you noticed?

- How comfortable are you with honestly looking at and confessing sin? How comfortable are you in accepting God's mercy and unconditional love?

- What is your level of inner freedom?

Ignatius hoped that by reflecting on sin and mercy that we would 1) be awakened to areas where we are not living out our created purpose and mourn that tragic reality and 2) be awakened to God's amazing mercy that helps us return to loving well. Both of these perspectives have the ultimate goal of filling us with deep longing to throw off all that hinders so that we eagerly pursue God's purpose for us. Has your journey through the First Week accomplished this? Talk with your spiritual director about where you are at.

SECOND WEEK

The Life of Jesus

Coming to Know Jesus

During the Principle and Foundation, we looked at God's love and purpose for us and all creation. During the First Week, we acknowledged the ways we are hindered in that meaningful purpose. Like Peter, we sometimes deny who we are and the Lord we love. We deny our own history—who God created us to be, our relationship with others, and the mission God has given us.[29] But, as Jesuit teacher of the Spiritual Exercises, Howard Gray, says, the Second Week is a reversal of Peter's denial of Jesus. The goal is to affirm all that we have denied. We affirm our identity, community, and mission. This affirmation is one of loyal friendship and devotion to Christ.

In the Second Week we enter the story of Jesus's life on earth. How does Jesus do ministry? In what ways does he cope with difficult circumstances? How does he depend on God? We see his vulnerability in infancy and his fatigue in ministry. We see his power, compassion, and authority as he heals and teaches. As we come to know and understand Jesus more (and thus God), we hear his invitation to join him in his work. That can stir excitement, but also reservations of what that might cost. This is a time of not only discerning what God is inviting us to in our lives, but also making concrete decisions concerning

---

[29] Per Howard Gray, SJ

those invitations.

As we move into the gospel narratives, we are also introduced to another major component of the Spiritual Exercises: *the shaping of the imagination.* Instead of analyzing Scripture as an intellectual exercise, we are invited to *experience* the stories of Jesus. During the Second Week you will practice imaginative contemplation and Scripture reading. The goal is to come to know Christ more deeply by entering into the stories as though we were there. We will walk alongside Jesus on dusty roads and witness his life and ministry.

Imagination and the Spiritual Life

The imagination profoundly shapes who we are and how we act. Our imagination is the world we live in, the way we perceive reality. It can guide us toward what is life-giving or what is destructive. The world projected by our imagination is fueled by whatever we drink in. We can imbibe the world through pornography or Facebook debates. Or we can choose to contemplate an autumn tree, the meaningful work of a non-profit organization, or the Gospel stories of Jesus.

Ignatius of Loyola became a follower of Jesus when he realized the effect of the imagination on his own life. He began to notice a significant difference when his mind was shaped by the stories of Jesus. The impact of filling his imagination with the things of God led him to radically change his life. He dedicated himself to ministry, even when it meant a lifetime of poverty and celibacy.

Similarly, Paul the Apostle wrote: "Finally, beloved, whatever is true, whatever is honorable, whatever is just, whatever is pure, whatever is pleasing, whatever is commendable, if there is any excellence and if there is anything worthy of praise, think about these things" (Phil 4:8). He went so far as to say we can be *transformed* by "renewing" our mind, and that the way we nurture our imagination has a direct impact on our ability to know the Divine will (Rom 12:2). The imagination is a determining factor in how we live our lives—for better or for worse.

In the digital age, it takes considerable discipline to proactively shape the imagination. Often it is easier to passively absorb whatever pops up on social media or Netflix. Studies have shown that we can even develop technology addictions that impact neurology and the way we relate to others.[30] Often we are unaware of how much we allow our imagination to be unpredictably and passively shaped. But we can take steps to proactively cultivate our imagination in beneficial ways.

Stories

The biblical authors often exhort us in the form of stories. Narratives have a way of enlarging our imagination. They help us to transcend present challenges to envision a world of possibility. As we see Jesus's compassion for the crowds and his healing touch, something stirs in our own spirit. Stories inspire us as we watch people living out the culture of the Kingdom in everyday life, whether the local school teacher pouring into her students or a couple pressing into faithfulness amid a challenging marriage. Similarly, fiction like *Lord of the Rings* or *Les Misérables* can also serve to turn our faces toward God. The world of these stories becomes our world until we, too, are living it out. We can actively shape our imagination by reading, hearing, or watching stories that stir our hearts to act with love.

Senses

One reason top geneticist Francis Collins converted from atheism to Christianity was the wonder of creation. Many people have experienced profound awe when standing before the Rocky Mountains or the Grand Canyon. Visual splendor can remind us of the grandeur of God. The same is true for the sound of ocean waves or music, the loving embrace of a friend, or the taste and smell of fresh food pulled from the earth. Some

---

[30] Hilarie Cash, et. al., "Internet Addiction: A Brief Summary of Research and Practice," *Current Psychiatry Reviews* 8 (2012): 292–298. http://www.ncbi.nlm.nih.gov/pmc/articles/PMC3480687/

of us grew up in traditions that told us to suppress our senses lest we be led astray, but God created us as embodied creatures. Our imagination can be quickened in positive ways through our senses.

Wisdom

Paul the Apostle lamented those who are "darkened in their understanding," leading to destructive living (Eph 4:17–24). Wisdom involves testing the spirits and not simply accepting anything and everything. It means questioning sources and engaging in critical thinking. Growing in wisdom often requires exposing ourselves to viewpoints that will challenge our presuppositions and stereotypes, and not just stay with whatever position feels most comfortable. We can shape our imagination by fact-checking. Such illumination gives us the ability to discern truth from lies, life from death, God's will from the will of the world.

Begin noticing and attending to your imagination. Reflect on how it affects your moods, attitudes, and actions. During the Spiritual Exercises, you will practice doing so by imaginatively entering the stories of Scripture. But consider how to give attention to the imagination as an on-going spiritual practice in your life beyond the Exercises.

Week 14
Anticipating the Kingdom

O God, help me to hear and understand what you are inviting me to participate in. Grant me an alertness to fulfill your will with my whole heart, soul, and mind.

Option 1

Prayer Practice: Pray the preparatory prayer:

Opening Prayer: Lord, please give me grace so that all my intentions and actions are focused solely on honoring and serving you.

Readying the Heart: Imagine the synagogues, towns, and villages where Jesus preached.

Request: Lord, help me to hear and understand what you are inviting me to participate in. Grant me an alertness to fulfill your will with my whole heart, soul, and mind.

Scripture: Luke 4:14–44.

Option 2

Reflection: "Contemplation of a Heroic Leader" (p. 94)

Option 3

Reflection: Think of a person or two that you admire because they wholeheartedly live out the ways of Jesus. Write down as many things you can think of about this person(s). What attributes do you appreciate the most? What kind of meaningful ways do they serve others? After you spend time thinking about this person(s), consider how those feelings of admiration can be transferred to Jesus. Consider that if you feel this way about an ordinary human being, how much more so of Jesus who is even greater.

Option 4
Scripture: Isaiah 40:1–11; Matthew 3:1–6
Reflection: Think of a specific area in your life where you desire personal transformation (perhaps something that came up during your reflections during the First Week). How might admiration for Jesus stir your heart toward change?

Option 5
Reflection: Watch and reflect on the documentary *Mary Mcleod Bethune—African Americans Who Left Their Stamp on History*. Bethune, a woman of faith, overcame significant hardships to help bring education to African American girls, as well as advance other social causes. How does Bethune remind you of Jesus? How might her life inspire you to pursue the work God has for you?

Option 6
Reading: "Reading Scripture with the Senses" (p. 97)
Scripture: Luke 1:26–56
Reflection: Contemplate Mary's yes to God's invitation in Luke's Gospel. Enter the story with your senses.

Reviewing the Week
Review the past week. What stands out to you the most as you have prayed and reflected on anticipating the Kingdom and Christ's invitation to you? Talk with God about your reflection.

Contemplation of a Heroic Leader

To foster feelings of admiration for Jesus whom we have not met in the flesh, Ignatius encouraged contemplation of a known praiseworthy leader. An emotional connection is made by association. We transfer the admiration we have for a leader we know to Jesus. For Ignatius, this association was made with a king (Ignatius had once served as a knight). The king had power, defended the people, and urged his knights to loyally serve the kingdom alongside him. But many people today have no personal experience with monarchies and perceive them differently than Ignatius did. For this contemplation exercise a modern-day heroic leader is suggested.

Part 1
Contemplate the life of Gary Haugen.

Gary grew up in Sacramento, California in a good Christian home without any initial aspirations to change the world.[31] Although he loved God, he lived a sheltered life fairly protected from global suffering. As a youngster, he dreamed of being a football player. However, Gary went on to become a lawyer and gradually was pierced by the pain he saw. In particular, his life changed in 1994 after being put in charge of the Rwandan genocide investigation. Three years later, he left the U.S. Department of Justice to create a new organization called International Justice Mission (IJM).

Since 1994, IJM has fought against oppression, rescuing people from slavery and violence. The organization employs more than 750 legal and social services professionals and has rescued more than 28,000 people around the world from forced

---

[31] Christian Buckley, "5 Good Minutes with Gary Haugen," http://www.conversantlife.com/social-justice/5-good-minutes-with-gary-haugen-%E2%80%93-founder-international-justice-mission

labor, sex trafficking, false imprisonment, and other forms of brutality—all because one man answered Jesus's invitation and encouraged others to join him.

Gary Haugen writes, "For Nagaraj and his family, who worked 16 hours a day, six days a week, making bricks, there was no mystery about what kept them and 80 other slaves inside the four walls of their compound. It was the vicious beatings unleashed upon those who tried to run away. For Elisabeth, a 16-year-old girl held inside a brothel in Thailand, it was money for Bible college that lured her into the hands of a sex trafficker who lied about a job across the border. Once inside the brothel, however, it was sheer violent terror that forced her to submit to multiple rapes by the brothel's paying customers."[32]

Haugen invites us to join the work: "Ultimately, this struggle to protect victims of violence and slavery is the work of God's kingdom. It is the Lord who commands us to 'seek justice, rescue the oppressed, defend the orphan, and plead for the widow' (Isa. 1:17), and it is Almighty God who promises to go with us as we declare to the Pharaohs of this world, 'Let my people go' (Ex. 5:1)."[33]

Part 2

After spending time contemplating the above, prayerfully ponder the following points and your own response.

1. *Consider that Jesus is greater than any earthly hero.* If an ordinary man like Gary Haugen might get our attention and convince us to join his vision, imagine how much more Jesus can capture our hearts.

---

[32] Gary Haugen, "On a Justice Mission," *Christianity Today*, Feb 2007, http://www.christianitytoday.com/ct/2007/march/16.40.html

[33] Haugen, "On a Justice Mission."

2. *Consider that such a hero would inspire the heart of any truly thoughtful and compassionate person.* She or he would want to find a way to be part of the good cause.

3. *Consider that a truly thoughtful and compassionate person might even go to great lengths,* actively giving up comfort and pleasure, to be part of Jesus's mission.

4. *What is your own response to Jesus's invitation?* Talk with God about it. One possibility could be expressed like this:

"Amazing God of all things, in light of your never-ending goodness, and before the witness of others, I offer my life to you. Empower me to embody that commitment. My earnest desire and decision is to imitate you, enduring whatever hardships or discomfort you may allow if that is necessary to serve you wholeheartedly."

Reading Scripture with the Senses

Ignatius of Loyola strongly desired to see integration between the heart and mind. He wanted us to read Scripture as if we were present with Jesus and not as detached observers analyzing the text. He understood the power of stories to shape the imagination and, therefore, our entire way of perceiving and being in the world. To facilitate entering the biblical narratives, he counseled the use of all our senses: sight, hearing, touch, taste, and smell. The following steps will help you begin to engage Scripture in this way.

1. Select a passage in Scripture that is *narrative*. The Bible has different genres. Narratives that depict scenes with detail are especially suited for using our senses and imagination. For the purposes of this Spiritual Exercises retreat the narratives have already been selected for you.

2. *Experience* the passage by reading it two or three times. Avoid analyzing the text. You are just drinking it in. Take in the sights and sounds. If it helps, listen to an audio version instead of reading. Ask God to bring illumination.

3. Close your eyes and play the scene in your mind like movie. Close the text, turn off the audio. Don't worry about checking to see if you "got it right." Just let the scene play out in your mind's eye. What do you see? What sounds or conversations do you hear? What are you touching? Is there anything to taste? What do you smell? As you engage your senses, consider the location, the type of people who are present, and interactions that are happening.

4. Reflect on where you are in the story. Envision yourself there with Jesus. What are you saying and doing in the scene? Is there a figure in the story that you identify with? What emotions are you experiencing?

5. Talk with God about the experience. What stands out to you the most? You can even talk with Jesus in the scene you are playing out. What is God saying to you? Are you being invited to take real-life action on anything?

Week 15:
The Incarnation, Infancy

O God, give me inner knowledge of you, who became human for me,
so that I might better love and follow you.

Option 1
Reflection: The word "incarnation" comes from a Latin term meaning embodied in flesh. It refers to God becoming a human being, taking on flesh and bone in the second Person of the Trinity, Jesus. Ponder the "Incarnation Contemplation" (p. 101)

Option 2
Reading: "Reflecting on Art for the Soul" (p. 102)
Art Reflection: Contemplate Henry Ossawa Tanner's painting "The Annunciation"—the scene where Gabriel appears to Mary (Luke 1:26–56).

Option 3
Scripture: Luke 2:1–20
Reflection: As you read the Scriptures, enter the story with your senses. What do you hear, see, taste, touch, smell? Imagine Mary and Joseph packing for the trip in Nazareth, the road to Bethlehem, the place of the nativity, conversations. Notice the humility of the situation. How is it that Christ was

"born in the greatest poverty; and after so many difficulties—of hunger, of thirst, of heat and of cold, of injuries and affronts—he died on the Cross; and all this for me" (*SE* 116)? Talk with God as you reflect on this.

Option 4

Reflection: Spend some time meditating on the words of "O Holy Night" (p. 103). What words, phrases, or images stand out to you the most? Talk with God about it. Afterward, sing the song as worship.

Option 5

Scripture: Philippians 2:6–11

Option 6

Scripture: John 1:1–18

Song: "O Come All Ye Faithful" or another favorite Christmas song.

Reflection: As you read this Scriptural passage, as well as contemplate and sing the song, what emotions or thoughts do you experience? Is there an integration between the heart and mind as you reflect on these materials in the Second Week? If so, what specific things stir you? If not, what might that be about?

Reviewing the Week

Look back on past week. What stands out to you the most as you have prayed and reflected on the Incarnation? Talk with God about your reflections

Incarnation Contemplation

Take a moment to ready your heart for this contemplation. Then take time to play these two scenes like a movie in your mind. Let your imagination bring you to these places. Afterward, close with the suggested prayer.

Scene 1: The three persons of the Trinity (Father, Son, and Spirit) are looking down on the earth filled with people "all in such variety, in dress as in actions: some white and others black; some in peace and others in war; some weeping and others laughing; some physically well, others ill; some being born and others dying" (*SE* 106). The Triune God sees all who are living in blindness and going to their deaths without hope. They hear the chatter of the people, the way they talk to each other, cursing and insulting. In unison, the Father, Son, and Spirit say: "Let us rescue humanity from its terrible plight!" They send the Son to become human. As the people on the earth harm and kill each other, the Triune God plans to bring about redemption through the Incarnation. At just the right moment they send the angel Gabriel to Mary.

Scene 2. In the Middle East, in the land of Judea, is the small town of Nazareth. In one humble home, Mary is alone for a moment when suddenly an angel appears. The angel speaks to her fantastic things beyond her wildest expectations. Mary is overwhelmed with a sense of humility and gratitude to God.

Closing Prayer: O God, give me inner knowledge of you who became human for me so that I might better love and follow you.

Have a conversation with the Triune God about any thoughts or feelings that came up during this Incarnation Contemplation. Close with the Our Father.

Reflecting on Art for the Soul

Throughout history, Christians have used art as a way to draw their imaginations into the story of God's relationship with humankind. In fact, icons have provided access to the biblical narratives for those who are illiterate. The world of art is wide and beautiful, leaving many possibilities for positive inspiration for those who want to incorporate art into the spiritual practice of shaping the imagination. When looking at art, such as a painting, ask God to show you something meaningful.

Set aside uninterrupted time to gaze and reflect on the art piece. Slowly take in the details. After an initial survey, you might even look at just one portion of the piece for a period of time. Consider the following questions as you reflect:

What colors do you see? What do they convey?

What do you notice about lines and tones?

What is in the foreground? What is in the background?

What relationships are depicted?

What emotions does the art draw from you?

Enter the story of this art piece with all your senses. Where are you in the story?

What stands out to you the most as you reflect? Why do you think that is? Talk with God about it.

O Holy Night
by Placide Cappeau[34]

O holy night! The stars are brightly shining,
It is the night of our dear Saviour's birth.
Long lay the world in sin and error pining,
Till He appear'd and the soul felt its worth.
A thrill of hope, the weary world rejoices,
For yonder breaks a new and glorious morn.

Fall on your knees! O hear the angel voices!
O night divine, O night when Christ was born;
O night divine, O night, O night Divine.

Led by the light of Faith serenely beaming,
With glowing hearts by His cradle we stand.
So led by light of a star sweetly gleaming,
Here come the wise men from the Orient land.
The King of Kings lay thus in lowly manger;
In all our trials born to be our friend.

He knows our need, to our weaknesses no stranger,
Behold your King! Before Him lowly bend!
Behold your King, Before Him lowly bend!

Truly He taught us to love one another;
His law is love and His gospel is peace.
Chains shall He break for the slave is our brother;
And in His name all oppression shall cease.

---

[34] Originally a poem, "Minuit, Chrétiens" (Midnight, Christians),
by Placide Cappeau. It was translated into English by John S. Dwight.
See *Gems of English Song: A Collection of Very Choice Songs, Duets and
Quartets; with an Accompaniment for the Piano-forte* (Boston: Oliver
Ditson, 1875), 206–208.

Sweet hymns of joy in grateful chorus raise we,
Let all within us praise His holy name.

Christ is the Lord! O praise His Name forever,
His power and glory evermore proclaim.
His power and glory evermore proclaim.

Week 16
The Incarnation, Childhood

*O God, give me inner knowledge of you, who became human for me,
so that I might better love and follow you.*

Option 1

Scripture: Luke 2:21–40

Reflection: Enter the story. What do you hear, taste, touch, see, smell? What do you notice about Mary's and Joseph's relationship with God? How might that have affected the way they raised Jesus?

Option 2

Scripture: Matthew 2:13–23

Reflection and Prayer: "Lord Jesus Christ, how intimately you desired to know us, starting among us as an infant, leaving nothing out. Your love ties you to us—even when some among us drive you away into all kinds of exile. But you keep coming back to your saints and holy ones. Lord, I say yes to your being here housed in our flesh." –Joseph A. Tetlow, SJ[35]

---

[35] Joseph A. Tetlow, *Choosing Christ in the World* (San Louis, The Institute for Jesuit Sources, 1999), 55.

Option 3

Activity: Observe a child or children (your own, a friend's, those at the park, etc). Imagine what Jesus was like at that age. Imagine God as a child.

Option 4

Scripture: Luke 2:41–52

Reflection: Enter the scene with all your senses. What is Jesus like?

Option 5

Art Reflection: "Jesus Among the Teachers" by Jesus Mafa (Luke 2:41–52)

Option 6

Reflection: Consider the Scriptures from this past week on Jesus's childhood. In what ways did Mary and Joseph yield to God's will? In what ways did Jesus honor God?

Reviewing the Week

Look back on the past week. What stands out to you the most as you have prayed and reflected on Jesus's childhood? Where is your own heart as you consider actively following God's purposes for your life in the way Jesus, Mary, and Joseph did? Talk with God about your reflections.

Week 17
Two Standards: God's Will vs. Temptation

Lord, I ask for discernment to recognize the evil spirit's deception and guard against it. Please enlighten my heart and mind to the true life revealed by Jesus and the grace to imitate him.

Option 1

Reflection: The story of Jesus begins before his birth when the second Person of the Trinity agrees to become a human being. The story continues in Mary's yes, as well as in Mary's and Joseph's obedience to the commandments of Torah. As a child, Jesus lives out submission to God. These provide models of obedience for our own lives. However, we all experience tension between the pull to follow God and the pull to acquiesce to the evil spirit. Whose banner (i.e. standard) will we ride under? Ponder the "Meditation on the Two Standards" (p. 109).

Option 2

Reading and Reflection: Ignatius asks us to imagine a very real spiritual struggle and to contrast Jesus's reign with that of the evil spirit's. He encourages us to be aware of the adversary's tactics by becoming more discerning. His imaginative exercise is quite similar to C.S. Lewis's *The Screwtape Letters*—letters of a chief demon to a junior demon about how to lure a human being away from God. Read letters (chapters) 4 & 12 of *The Screwtape Letters*.

Option 3

Reading and Reflection: Reflect on letter (chapter) 14 of *The Screwtape Letters*.

Option 4

Re-read: "Making Sense of Inner Spiritual Movement."[36]

Closing Prayer: The Examen, paying particular attention to movements toward or away from God.

Option 5

Scripture: 1 Peter 5:8–9

Close with the Examen

Option 6

Scripture: Ephesians 6:10–18

Close with Examen

Reviewing the Week

Look back on the past week. What stands out to you the most as you have prayed and reflected concerning the Two Standards and the evil spirit's deception? What spiritual struggles do you notice in your own life? Be specific. Talk with God about your reflections.

---

[36] Chapter 5 in *What's Your Decision?*

Meditation on the Two Standards

Begin with a preparatory prayer to ready your heart for the meditation. Then take some time to play these scenes like a movie in your mind. Let your imagination bring you to these places. Afterward, close with the suggested prayer.

Setting: Jesus, Lord of all that is good, stands in a plain desiring and calling everybody to be under his standard (i.e. banner). Simultaneously, the evil spirit stands in a different plain and his voice is heard calling everyone to be under his standard.

Scene 1: The evil spirit is standing in a great plain in the region of "Babylon" — a place of terror, contempt, pollution, and pain. The adversary is using his power to harm and influence human beings. He summons spiritual forces and sends them to cities around the world, infiltrating every place. The evil spirit speaks to the demons under his authority and tells them to ensnare people. He commands the evil powers to tempt people to greed, coveting, empty honors, and pride. The adversary tempts all human beings to place value and identity in anything except God.

Scene 2: The Ruler of All, Jesus Christ our Lord, is standing in the region of "Jerusalem" — a place of beauty, kindness, healing, and peace. The Lord chooses many people — disciples — and sends them throughout the world to spread the good news of freedom to every people in every nation and in every condition. Jesus speaks to his followers urging them to help all women and men by drawing them to the things of God, especially humility. Out of humility come all the other fruit of the Spirit. Jesus is heard saying, "Blessed are the poor in spirit. Blessed are those that find their identity and meaning in God and not worldly things." Jesus urges his followers to help others who have been trapped by the evil spirit.

Closing Prayer: Lord, I ask for discernment to recognize the evil spirit's deception and guard against it. Please enlighten my heart and mind to the true life revealed by Jesus and the grace to imitate him. May I be filled with a spirit of humility and endurance to face hardship for the sake of your Kingdom.

Week 18
Two Standards, Part 2

Lord, I ask for discernment to recognize the evil spirit's deception and guard against it. Please enlighten my heart and mind to the true life revealed by Jesus and the grace to imitate him.

Option 1

Scripture: I John 4:1–4

Reflection: Revisit scene 2 in the "Meditation on the Two Standards" (p. 109). Spend some time reflecting on the reality that greater is the One who is in you than the one who is in the world.

Option 2

Scripture: Matthew 4:1–11

Reflection: Enter the scene with all your senses. What do you notice about the way Jesus responds to the adversary? What aspects might you imitate this week for confronting your own spiritual battles?

Option 3

Activity: Meet with (or phone) someone today, a friend or pastor, and risk sharing vulnerably about spiritual struggles you experience in your life. Honesty frees us from the evil spirit's power.

Option 4

Scripture: Mark 1:16–20

Reflection: Drink in this scene. Then set the text aside and draw a picture of what you visualize in your mind. Don't worry about making it perfect. It can be life-like or symbolic. Draw what comes to the surface for you. Where are you in the picture?

Option 5

Reading and reflection: "Ignatius's Rules for Discernment of Spirits"[37]

Option 6

Scripture: Reflect again on Mark 1:16–20

Reviewing the Week

Look back on the past week. What stands out to you the most as you have prayed and reflected on the Two Standards and Christ's work? Talk with God about your reflections.

---

[37] Chapter 6 in *What is Your Decision?*

Week 19
Humility, Simplicity, and Inner Freedom

Kind Spirit, fill me with humility, simplicity, and inner freedom.
Give me the ability to let go of anything to which I am clinging too
tightly, and a willingness to endure challenges
for the sake of serving you.

Option 1

Scripture: Matthew 5:1–12

Reflection: What do you notice about the kind of person Jesus is from the Beatitudes? These are the signs of a follower of Christ. Do you recognize yourself in them?

Option 2

Scripture: Repeat Matthew 5:1–12

Reflection: Of all the Beatitudes, which one do you long for most right now? Ask God what that would look like on a practical level. Pray for ideas about how you can begin taking action this week.

Option 3

Ponder the "Three Types of People Meditation" (p. 115).

Option 4

Scripture: Luke 12:13–34

Reflection: What do you notice about themes of inner freedom and the lack of it?

Option 5

Scripture: Luke 21:1–4

Activity: Engage in the spiritual practice of inner freedom. Pray about something of significant value that you will choose to give away today or in the next few days (it could be time, possession, money, etc). Something that costs you, but benefits another. Talk with God about your experience.

Option 6

Reading and reflection: "Rules for Subtle Discernment"[38]

Reviewing the Week

Look back on the past week. What stands out to you the most as you have prayed and reflected on the characteristics of Jesus's Standard? Consider the contrasts between what it means to be a friend and disciple of Jesus vs. a disciple of the evil spirit. In what areas are you pulled toward the values of God? In what ways are you pulled toward the values of the adversary? Are there specific decisions you need to make (even minor daily ones) to commit to Jesus's Standard? Talk with God about your reflections.

---

[38] Chapter 7 in *What's Your Decision?*

Three Types of People Meditation

Begin with a preparatory prayer to ready your heart for the following meditation.

Scene: You are standing next to God along with many other devout people. Your heart is eager, hoping to grow in desire and knowledge of what is most pleasing to God. To give you spiritual illumination, you are shown three different types of people. All of them have come to possess a good amount of money. And each one wants to handle their wealth in a godly way. They want to let go of any obsessive attachment to money that might negatively impact their relationship with God.

- The first person wants freedom, but she makes no effort to use her money for God's purposes until the time of her death. She just never got around to seriously talking to God about it.

- The second person wants greater inner freedom, and he is willing to act now to employ his money. But he is not fully free. Instead of asking what God wants, he prays that God will bless the decisions he has already made about the money. He is not fully open to other Spirit-led possibilities. Therefore, he does not have the inner freedom necessary to make whatever decision God might inspire.

- The third person also desires inner freedom, but unlike the second person she is willing to approach the money with open palms. She neither wishes for it to be taken from her nor hopes to keep it. All she wants is for her desires (whether to keep it or give it away) to be whatever God wants. She has achieved inner freedom because she is not overly attached to the thing. She desires neither a rich life nor a poor life, but only what will allow her to serve God best. As a result of this inner freedom, she is truly free to make a Spirit inspired decision.

As you meditate on these three responses and the varying levels of inner freedom, consider your own life. What are your attachments? They could be related to any number of things and not just money. In what areas are you more like one of the above three than the other?

Closing Prayer
Lord, help me to make decisions that glorify you and are congruent with your redemptive work.

Note: Keep in mind that inner freedom is not an attempt to eradicate desire. We can strongly desire something and still be willing to do whatever God asks. Inner freedom is an openness of heart.

Week 20
Getting to Know Jesus, Part 1

*O God, give me inner knowledge of you who became human for me
so that I might better love and follow you.*

Option 1

Re-read: "Reading Scripture with the Senses" (p. 97)

Scripture: Luke 8:40-56

Reflection: Enter the scene in the Scripture reading. What is Jesus like? How does he respond to what is happening around him? What motivates him?

Option 2

Scripture: Luke 9:46–62

Reflection: Enter the scene. What is Jesus like? How does he interact with people? What does it mean to follow him?

Option 3

Scripture: Luke 11:29–54

Reflection: Enter the scene? What does Jesus care about? Where are you in the story? How do you react to what he is saying?

Option 4

Art Reflection: "Healing of the Bent Woman" (Luke 13:10–21) by Dmitry Shkolnik

Option 5

Scripture: Luke 15:1–10

Activity: Drink in the text. Then draw a picture of Jesus. What image do you have of him?

Option 6

Repeat any of the days from this week.

Reviewing the Week:

Look back on the past week. What stands out to you the most as you have sought to know the person of Jesus better? Talk with God about your reflections.

Song: "Give Me Jesus" by Fernando Ortega or another worship song that helps you to know Jesus.

Week 21
Getting to Know Jesus, Part 2

O God, give me inner knowledge of you who became human for me so that I might better love and follow you.

Option 1

Scripture: Mark 3

Reflection: Place yourself in the scene. Act it out either with someone else or by yourself. Who does Jesus choose for his inner circle of disciples? How come? What does he expect of them?

Option 2

Scripture: John 4:1–38

Reflection: Enter the scene. Continue to contemplate what kind of person Jesus is and what it means to associate with him as friend and disciple. Who do *you* tend to view as a Samaritan in your community? In what ways are you prepared to imitate Jesus's example here? In what ways do you hold back?

Option 3

Reflection: As you have been getting to know Jesus, where do you recognize him in daily life?

Close with the Examen as a way of noticing the Spirit of Christ in the here and now.

Option 4

Activity: Contemplate what you have observed about Jesus so far. Find something to imitate that you have seen and act on it today. Embodying what Jesus does can help us to know him better.

Option 5

Scripture: Mark 10

Reflection: Of these various scenes, what one stands out the most? Act it out either with someone else or by yourself. Where are you in it?

Option 6

Art Reflection: "Triumphant Entry into Jerusalem" (Mark 11) by He Qi.

Reviewing the Day:

Look back on the past week. What stands out to you the most as you have sought to know the person of Jesus better? Talk with God about your reflections.

Week 22
Getting to Know Jesus, Part 3

O God, give me inner knowledge of you who became human for me
so that I might better love and follow you.

Option 1
Scripture: John 11:1–46
Reflection: Enter the scene. Consider how Jesus is both human and divine. In what ways does Jesus's humanity show up? Where do you see his divinity?

Option 2
Scripture: John 8:1–11
Reflection: Continue to ponder Jesus's humanity and divinity.

Option 3
Reflection: Spend some time praying and contemplating what you have come to know about Jesus these last few weeks. How does the Incarnation help you to see what it means for *you* to be fully human? How does Jesus's humanity offer an accessible example for you to follow?

Option 4

Scripture: John 5:16–23

Reflection: In what ways does Jesus depend on the Father? How might this be an encouragement when you feel inadequate for God's work?

Option 5

Art Reflection: "The Calling of St. Matthew" by Michelangelo Merisi da Caravaggio (Matthew 9:9–13; see also Zacchaeus in Luke 19:1-10).

Option 6

Scripture: Repetition of any of the days from this week.

Reviewing the Week

Look back on the past week. What stands out to you the most as you have sought to know the person of Jesus better? Talk with God about your reflections.

Song: "Come to Jesus" by Chris Rice or a favorite hymn on the life of Jesus.

Week 23
Making a Decision in Freedom

Kind Spirit, fill me with humility, simplicity, and inner freedom.
Give me the ability to let go of anything to which I am clinging too
tightly, and a willingness to endure challenges
for the sake of serving you.

Option 1

Reflection: Revisit and talk with God concerning "Meditation on the Two Standards" (p. 109) and the "Three Types of People Meditation" (p. 115). Recall that the first meditation helps us to consider the contrast between two authorities, that of Jesus and that of the evil spirit. The second one helps us to consider degrees of inner freedom, and the reality that we need freedom from inordinate attachments to be truly open to making decisions that honor God. Where are you at? Be specific. It may help to journal as you pray.

Option 2

Scripture: John 21:15–23

Reflection: The Second Week is a reversal of the ways we have denied our created purpose. Or in other words, how we have denied Christ. For the three times Peter denied Jesus, Jesus asked him "Do you love me?" Spend some time on this passage and what it means for your life. In what concrete ways in daily life do you deny Jesus? In what concrete ways do you love him?

Option 3
Reflection: Contemplate the "Three Kinds of Humility" (p. 125).

Option 4
Reading and reflection: "Decision Making in Mode 1: 'No Doubt about It" and "Decision Making in Mode 2: Spiritual Movements."[39]

Option 5
Reading and reflection: "Decision Making in Mode 3: Calm Deliberation."[40]

Option 6
Reflection: What concrete decisions are on the horizon for you? Spend some time journaling or drawing about these potential decisions.

Reviewing the Week
Review the past week. What stands out as you have considered what it means to make decisions to follow Christ in daily life? Talk with God about your reflections.

Close with "O God, What Offering Shall I Give?" by Joachim Lange (p. 127).

---

[39] Chapters 9 and 10 in *What's Your Decision?* Chapter 9 is only a few pages so I have combined it with chapter 10 for this day's reflection.

[40] Chapter 11 in *What's Your Decision?*

Three Kinds of Humility

The first kind of humility involves humbly submitting as much as I am able to God's will in everything. This humility is such that even if I was given great power over all created things or my life was at stake, I would not make any decision that would go against God's will. Thus, the first humility is characterized by obedience to God's authority.

The second kind of humility involves a disposition and willingness to live with open palms. I neither "want health more than sickness, riches more than poverty, honor more than dishonor, a long life more than a short life, and so in all the rest; desiring and choosing only what most helps us toward the end for which we are created" (*SE* 23). The second humility is especially characterized by inner freedom. It is also better than the first humility as it includes both the characteristics of the first as well as the second. Thus, the second humility comprises obedience and inner freedom.

The third kind of humility is the greatest kind. It includes obedience and inner freedom, but also has an additional characteristic: intentionally choosing hardship rather than pleasures in order to imitate Christ most fully. It includes willingness to be a fool for Christ rather than esteemed by others. The third humility is self-sacrifice regardless of the cost—discomfort, poverty, ridicule, or death. Thus, the third humility comprises obedience, inner freedom, and self-sacrifice.

All such humility is motivated by deep love. As Jesus said, there is no greater love than to lay down one's life for a friend. Such submission to God, availability, and endurance are motivated entirely from being in love with God and not fear or legalism.

Closing prayer: Lord, though I am weak and frail, I love you and want to love you more. Empower me to yield fully to your will, to live with open palms so as to discern and follow your guidance wherever it leads, and to have courage to live self-sacrificially. Give me a heart of submission to you, availability, and endurance. Give me a heart of true humility.

O God, What Offering Shall I Give?

By Joachim Lange[41]

O God, what offering shall I give
To you, the Lord of earth and skies?
My spirit, soul, and flesh receive,
A holy, living sacrifice;
Small as it is, 'tis all my store;
More should you have, if I had more.

Now then, my God, you have my soul,
No longer mine, but yours I am;
Guard your own, possess it whole,
Cheer it with hope, with love inflame;
You have my spirit, there display
Your glory to the perfect day.

You have my body, your holy shrine,
Devoted solely to your will;
Here let your light forever shine,
This house still let your presence fill;
O Source of life, live, dwell, and move
In me, till all my life be love!

O never in these veils of shame,
Sad fruits of sin, my glorying be!
Clothe with salvation, through your name,
My soul, and let me put on you!
Be living faith my costly dress,
And my best robe your righteousness.

---

[41] Adapted slightly from Joachim Lange's 1697 hymn "O Jesu, Süsses Licht," translated by John Wesley in *Wesleyan Hymn Book* (1780), no. 419.

Send down your likeness from above,
And let this my adorning be;
Clothe me with wisdom, patience, love,
With lowliness and purity,
Than gold and pearls more precious far,
And brighter than the morning star.

Lord, arm me with your Spirit's might,
Since I am called by your great name;
In you let all my thoughts unite,
Of all my works be you the aim;
Your love attend me all my days,
And my sole business be your praise!

Week 24
Reviewing the Journey

You have now completed the Second Week, covering these themes:

- Imagination and the spiritual life
- Anticipating the Kingdom
- Getting to know and admire Jesus
- Two Standards (to whose authority will you submit?)
- Discerning the spirits
- Humility and simplicity
- Inner freedom (continued)
- Making decisions

You have also been introduced to these practices:

- Reading Scripture with the senses
- Reflecting on art for the soul
- Imaginative contemplations/meditations
    -Contemplation of a Heroic Leader
    -Incarnation Contemplation
    -Meditation on the Two Standards
    -Three Types of People Meditation
    -Three Kinds of Humility

Before moving on to the Third Week, take the next several days to contemplate your experience of the Second Week. Look back over your journal and other sign posts. Ask God to bring to the surface what is most important for your spiritual process. As you reflect, keep prayer at the center (not just an intellectual or meditative review). The goal is always connection with God.

- What emotions and desires arise as you reflect on your experience of the Second Week?

- What stands out to you the most? (e.g. Recurring patterns? Specific images or Scriptures?)

- In what ways has your imagination been shaped during the Second Week?

- What is something you have discovered about Jesus that you didn't notice before? How does it affect you?

- What are practical ways you can imitate Jesus based on what you observed and experienced of him during these past weeks? How might you begin acting on these today?

- How is it going with practicing spiritual discernment and decision-making?

- What have you noticed about interior movements and actions toward or away from God, especially as it relates to the Two Standards?

- How are your conversations with God? Are there things you have not talked with God about? Are there certain ways of praying that you have found helpful?

- Are there particular areas you want to spend more time on? What do you hope for as you continue?

The Second Week is designed to give us a more intimate experience of Jesus. As we get to know him better, we gain an understanding of what it means to imitate the ways of God. We also begin to sense what that might look like for our own lives. The Second Week hones our ability to discern and make decisions that proactively respond to Jesus's invitation to join God's work. Where are you at on these things? Be sure to talk with your spiritual director about your reflections.

Close with this excerpt from St. Patrick's hymn.[42]

Christ with me, Christ before me,
Christ behind me, Christ within me,
Christ beneath me, Christ above me,
Christ at my right, Christ at my left.

Christ in the heart of every man who thinks of me,
Christ in the mouth of every man who speaks to me,
Christ in every eye that sees me,
Christ in every ear that hears me.

---

[42] This translation from English is from James Henthorn Todd, *St. Patrick: Apostle of Ireland* (Dublin: Hodges, Smith, and Co., 1864), 428. The hymn is commonly believed to have been written by St. Patrick, though we don't have definitive proof.

THIRD WEEK

Going to the Cross with Jesus

Going to the Cross with Jesus

If you have reached the Third Week of the Spiritual Exercises, you have made the decision to go with Jesus to the cross. There are two primary aspects to this Week: compassion for Jesus's suffering (and that of others) and coming to terms with one's own suffering and death. First, we walk the road from Bethany to Jerusalem where we witness the Last Supper, the betrayal of our dear friend, and like Mary Magdalene and John risk going all the way to sit where Jesus hangs in agony. As we watch Jesus suffer and die, we grow in our capacity to empathize with another person's suffering. We also become painfully aware of how sin contributed to this tragedy and marvel that Jesus voluntarily endured it for a greater good.

Second, we pick up our own cross. As disciples, we follow our Lord's example, giving our lives for the sake of others. This is not easy. Like Jesus we pray, "Take this cup from me." But, as we are inspired by Christ's decision, we gain courage to say, "Yet not my will, but Your will be done." Significantly, God's will is never suffering just for the sake of suffering. Jesus didn't volunteer to die because of a "martyr's complex." In fact, God anointed Jesus for the specific purpose of eliminating suffering (Acts 10:38). Taking up our cross is for the sake of helping others.

The disposition of this Week is sorrow—the kind of sadness

that comes when we care about and empathize with the pain of another. Ignatius suggests we engage in acts of lament, including fasting or abstaining from delicacies or other pleasures. At the same time, this Week is also intended to cultivate resilience, that is, to strengthen our decision to follow Christ as we imitate him, setting our faces "like flint" toward Jerusalem (Luke 9:51).

Week 25

The Walk to Jerusalem

O God, please give me the ability to empathize with Jesus's grief,
as well as the suffering of others. Grant me strength
and courage to follow his example.

Option 1

Scripture: Matthew 26:6–13

Reflection: Enter the scene with your senses. Contemplate your daily life: in what specific ways are you like the disciples? In what ways are you like the woman?

Option 2

Reflection: "Bethany to Jerusalem Contemplation" (p. 139)

Option 3

Reflection: Meditate on the story of Sophie Scholl who knowingly pursued a mission that would likely (and did) result in her death (see "Supplements" at website). Ponder how Jesus similarly knew he was risking death for a purpose. Where is your own heart at?

Option 4

Scripture: John 13:1–20

Reflection: Place yourself in the scene. Play it out like a movie in your mind. What seems to motivate Jesus to make this gesture of foot washing at this pivotal time? How does it feel to have Jesus wash your feet?

Option 5

Scripture: Luke 22:24–27

Reflection: Ponder this scene in light of Jesus's foot washing at the same meal. Where are you in the story?

Option 6

Scripture: Come back to John 13:1–20 and read it two or three times. As you do, notice what specific words or phrases stand out to you. What might God be speaking to you?

Reviewing the Week

Look back on the past week. What stands out to you the most as you have prayed and reflected on the days before Jesus's arrest? Talk with God about your reflections.

Bethany to Jerusalem Contemplation

Begin with a preparatory prayer to ready your heart for the contemplation. Take some time to play each scene like a movie in your mind. Let your imagination bring you to these places. Afterward, close with the suggested prayer.

Scene 1: Jesus has just been anointed for burial by the woman in Bethany. While still there he sends two disciples ahead of him to Jerusalem to prepare the Last Supper. Then he and the other disciples begin the walk from Bethany. Picture the road. The skyline. What do you see, hear, taste, touch, smell?

Scene 2. After Jesus arrives, they eat the Passover lamb. Picture the room. Hear him speak of the bread and wine. See him washing the disciples' feet. Listen to the conversation while Judas slips out to betray him.

Scene 3. Imagine Jesus's arrest, torture, and crucifixion. Draw on all your emotions to grieve and sorrow over this event. Consider how Jesus does not retaliate against his enemies who abuse him, but allows himself to suffer in this terrible way.

Scene 4. Consider how Jesus voluntarily suffered because of sin as well. Watch him hanging on the cross on your behalf. Contemplate what difficult, but purposeful service you might give to him in return. Be specific.

Closing Prayer: O God, please give me the ability to empathize with Jesus's suffering and grief, as well as the pain of others. Grant me strength and courage to follow his example.

Week 26
Final Days

O God, please give me the ability to empathize with Jesus's grief,
as well as the suffering of others. Grant me strength
and courage to follow his example.

Option 1

Scripture: Mark 14:22–31

Reflection: Enter the scene. Jesus speaks of his death and how his friends will leave him at his most vulnerable moment. Cultivate empathy for Jesus. Ponder an incident in your own life or someone you know who was abandoned at a critical time. Then transfer those feelings to this biblical scene.

Option 2

Scripture: John 6:35–69

Reflection: Similar to themes in Mark 14, in this passage many disciples leave. Enter the story. How do you respond? What fears or discomfort do you have related to being a disciple?

Option 3

Reflection: Watch the movie *Of Gods and Men* based on a true story of Trappist monks in Algeria. Pay particular attention to the scene modeled after the Last Supper (toward the end of the movie). What emotions are portrayed? How does this movie help you to have compassion for Jesus's fate while also helping you to reflect on what it means to die with him?

Option 4

Repetition or reflection on any of the previous days this week.

Option 5

Activity: Spend some extended time praying for someone you know is going through a hard time. Ask God to give you empathy and insight on how you might be present for this person in a concrete way (e.g. sending a card, making a meal, inviting them to hang out, giving a hug, etc).

Option 6

Scripture: Mark 14:32–42

Reflection: Enter the scene with your senses. Empathize with Jesus's experience in the garden of Gethsemane. Consider his humanity.

Activity: Think of someone in your community in need of emotional support right now. Reach out to that person as if you were reaching out to Jesus in Gethsemane. Keep in mind that often quiet presence and "keeping watch" is most needed and not "fix it" advice.

Reviewing the Week

Look back on the past week. What stands out to you the most as you have prayed and reflected on the days before Jesus's arrest? Talk with God about your reflections.

Week 27
Arrest and Crucifixion

O God, please give me the ability to empathize with Jesus's grief,
as well as the suffering of others. Grant me strength
and courage to follow his example.

Option 1

Scripture: Mark 14:43–15:21

Reflection: Enter the scene. This is your best friend. You are one of his disciples watching all of this happening. What are you feeling? How do you respond?

Option 2

Reflection: Meditate on the story of Anthony Ray Hinton, an innocent man who spent 30 years on death row in a tiny cell after being falsely accused (p. 144). Consider the feelings of helplessness and anguish at having one's life stolen by people in power. How might you empathize with Jesus in people who are unfairly arrested and incarcerated today?

Option 3

Reflection: Think of the person you love most. Imagine that you know your loved one's death is imminent. Or recall a time when you lost such a loved one. What do you want to say to this person before he or she dies? Let the feelings you experience be transferred to what it would be like watching Jesus about to die.

Activity: Today, do something for someone to express how much they mean to you.

Option 4

Scripture: Mark 15:22–41

Reflection: Watch Jesus die. Grieve for and with him. Consider how ISIS crucified people (images can be found online: viewer discretion advised).[43] What do you feel as you reflect on a modern example? Let these victims be Christ to you as you consider Jesus's crucifixion.

Option 5

Scripture: John 19:16–30

Reflection: Watch Jesus die. Grieve for and with him. Consider who is there with him and who is not. Honestly reflect on where your own heart is at.

Option 6

Scripture: Mark 8:34–38; Romans 6:1–7; Romans 12:1–2ff

Reflection: What would it look like in your life to pick up your cross and die with Christ? Be practical, concrete, and specific. What emotions arise for you as you contemplate this?

Song: "Crown of Thorns" by Danielle Rose or another worship song about living self-sacrificially.

Reviewing the Week

Look back on the past week. What stands out to you the most as you have prayed and reflected on Jesus's arrest and execution? Talk with God about your reflections.

---

[43] Use your discernment about looking at images. You are under no obligation to do so.

Jesus's Arrest and Anthony Ray Hinton

Imagine living day in and day out in a closet or a space the size of a small bathroom. With only six by nine feet to move and no ability to leave, what would you do hour after hour, month after month? That was Anthony Ray Hinton's reality for thirty years while he sat on death row for a crime he didn't commit. With the COVID-19 pandemic, many of us experienced the challenge of limited mobility and social contact. But that was nothing in comparison to the agonizing confinement Hinton experienced. How does a human being live in a tiny, concrete box for thirty years and come out sane?

Born in Alabama, Hinton was the youngest of ten siblings raised by a single mom. He had a close relationship with his mother and was living with her when, at the age of 29, he was violently taken from his relatively tranquil life and thrown in prison. Hinton did not even know about the murders that had taken place fifteen miles away while he worked his graveyard shift at a warehouse—his employers kept the building locked and required employees to clock in. Yet despite his clear alibi, he did not see freedom again for three decades.

Hinton was subjected to the torture of living on death row while racist officials rigged the system. The authorities wanted a scapegoat, someone to appease the public in the face of the murders. They did not care who did it. A prosecutor even admitted that he judged Hinton not so much on evidence, but by his appearance, which he deemed "evil." Hinton is black. Even after three of the nation's top firearm experts testified that the bullets found at the murder scenes could not be matched to a revolver stored (unused) in Hinton's mother's house, authorities tried to cover their mistake by keeping Hinton on death row for thirteen more years.

While he was in prison, Hinton's mother, who prayed every day for her son's release, died without being able to see him freed. He was not able to attend her funeral or care for her as he had been doing before he was unjustly arrested and imprisoned. Only after the relentless work of attorney Bryan Stevenson, was Anthony Ray Hinton exonerated and released in 2015. But freedom was bittersweet; nothing could restore the years taken from him or remedy the trauma inflicted.

Jesus said that whatever we do to the "least of" our fellow human beings we are doing to him (Matt 25:31–46). In Hinton, we see Christ's arrest all over again. We see the same false accusations, unjust trial, torture, and death sentence. As we contemplate Jesus's arrest, we do not recall a distant tragedy, we reflect on how injustice continues today. Jesus's face can be seen in Anthony Ray Hinton and the countless other men and women who have suffered under corruption within the criminal justice system.[44]

---

[44] For more on Anthony Ray Hinton, see his memoir, *The Sun Does Shine: How I Found Life and Freedom on Death Row* (2018).

Week 28
Grieving Death

*O God, please give me the ability to empathize with Jesus's grief,
as well as the suffering of others. Grant me strength
and courage to follow his example.*

Option 1

Activity: Find a location that hosts the Stations of the Cross
and prayerfully contemplate the scenes. If one is not available,
create your own Stations of the Cross.

Option 2

Reflection: Recall a time when you sacrificed something
important or made a painful decision, yet did so with a
conviction that it was the right thing. What present or future
difficult sacrifices do you face? What motivates you to consider
making them? Talk with God about it.

Option 3

Scripture: Luke 23:50–56

Reflection: Your best friend is gone. Now the body has to be
handled. Enter the scene. Where are you in it? What do you
notice? What emotions arise? Consider any experiences you
have had with loss, burial, or being present with a dead body
of someone you know.

Option 4

Activity: Think of someone you know who is grieving the loss of a loved one (sometimes this can be long after a death and not only immediately). Spend some time in prayer for them. Cultivate feelings of empathy for that person. Ask God if there is something you might do to be present for him or her.

Option 5

Scripture: "They stood still, looking sad. Then one of them, whose name was Cleopas, answered him, 'Are you the only stranger in Jerusalem who does not know the things that have taken place there in these days?' He asked them, 'What things?' They replied, 'The things about Jesus of Nazareth, who was a prophet mighty in deed and word before God and all the people, and how our chief priests and leaders handed him over to be condemned to death and crucified him. But we had hoped that he was the one to redeem Israel. Yes, and besides all this, it is now the third day since these things took place.'"[45]

Reflection: Slowly contemplate this scene like a movie. Enter the story. Let the grief and disappointment of these days following Jesus's death sink in.

Option 6

Repeat any of the previous days this week.

Reviewing the Week

Look back on the past week. What stands out to you the most as you have prayed and reflected on Jesus's death and the days immediately after? Talk with God about your reflections.

---

[45] From Luke 24:17–21. At this time, do not read the context as Luke 24 takes the story beyond the crucifixion. It's important to stay in the moment of this time of grieving Jesus's death.

Week 29
Reviewing the Journey

You have completed the Third Week, covering the following:

- Sorrow and compassion for Jesus's suffering
- Spiritual practice of empathizing with others
- Coming to terms with one's own suffering and death
- Greater willingness to suffer hardship for sake of advancing God's good work.

You also practiced:
- Imaginative contemplation
     -Bethany to Jerusalem Contemplation

Before moving on to the Fourth Week, take the next several days to contemplate your experience of the Third Week. Look back over your journal and other sign posts. Ask God to bring to the surface what is most important for your spiritual process. As you reflect, keep prayer at the center (not just an intellectual or meditative review). The goal is always connection with God.

- What emotions and desires arise as you reflect on your experience of the Third Week?

- What stands out to you the most? (e.g. Recurring patterns? Specific images or Scriptures?)

- What is something you have discovered about Jesus that you didn't notice before? How does it affect you?

- What are practical ways you can imitate Jesus's self-sacrifice? Where do you find it difficult to do so?

- Where are you at in your ability to empathize with others, including those who are difficult to love or that you don't know well?

- How has your prayer been going? Are you talking openly with God during your retreat time about what you are experiencing? What kind of things is the Holy Spirit impressing on you?

Before we are truly free to do whatever God might invite us to do, we need to be willing to die with Christ. As we empathize with the suffering of Jesus and others, we begin to see that our endurance of hardship is not for the sake of an abstract "martyr complex." Rather, we sacrifice ourselves to foster goodness and well-being for others. We cease to care only for our own comfort and desires, and widen our hearts to include the needs of those around us. Do you feel the Third Week has accomplished its purpose? Talk with your spiritual director about where you are at.

FOURTH WEEK

Resurrection and Reunion

Resurrection and Reunion

Joy! That is the mood of the Fourth Week. We rejoice not merely in the single event of the resurrection, but also the powerful life of Jesus that is still active today. Throughout the Exercises, Ignatius has always had the Risen Jesus in mind. Perhaps that is why he does not provide a meditation specifically on the Resurrection event itself. Instead, he leads us to contemplate the many interactions Jesus had during his forty days on earth after the resurrection and before his ascension into heaven. These encounters were transformative. They changed the way his friends understood and viewed reality. Similarly, we can meet the Risen Jesus in our own lives.

At the beginning of this retreat we were reminded of our created purpose and the things that can hinder us from that. By the end, we come to understand how God frees and empowers us. Sin may have cosmic dimensions, but far surpassing still are the cosmic effects of the gifts and life of God. The joy of this reality "has the typical effects of consolation. Consolation always moves a person to God's service."[46] The Fourth Week ends with the Contemplation to Attain Love (*Contemplatio*). This is an expansion and deepening of the Principle and Foundation. It emphasizes our union with

---

[46] Ivens, *Understanding*, 162.

God. This mutual love fills us with gratitude so that we serve others out of affection and not obligation.

During this week, cultivate feelings of joy and thanksgiving. Ignatius suggests such things as delighting in the particular pleasures of the season such as sunshine (if warm outside) or a cozy fire (if cold). Fill your heart and mind with celebration and gratitude.

> "Our Lord has written the promise of resurrection,
> not in books alone, but in every leaf in springtime."

> –Unknown[47]

---

[47] This quote is often attributed to Martin Luther. But there is no record of it.

Week 30
Resurrection Stories, Part 1

Spirit of Life, fill me with gladness and joy to celebrate Jesus the Lord who is alive today and invites me into relationship and collaborative mission.

Option 1

Scripture: Matthew 28:1–10

Reflection: Think of someone you love dearly that you have not seen in a long time. Daydream about a reunion. Then enter this biblical scene with all your senses. Notice Jesus's appearance to the women (vv. 9–10). What is everyone feeling? Where are you in the story?

Option 2

Reflection: Watch the reunion of a father with his small son. He believed his child died in a bombing (see video on "Supplements" page at website). How might this scene be similar to reactions to Jesus's unexpected resurrection?

Option 3

Reflection: Ponder the "Contemplation of Jesus's Appearance to His Mother"[48] (p. 157)

---

[48] Even though Scripture does not recount Jesus's meeting with his mother, there is no doubt she would have been one of the first to see him. Ignatius asks us to imagine him appearing to her first.

Option 4

Activity: Throw a Resurrection Party! Celebrate. Ask people to share where they have seen and experienced resurrection in their life.

Option 5

Scripture: John 20:1–18

Reflection: Enter the scene with all your senses. What do you notice about the reunion between Jesus and Mary Magdalene?

Option 6

Repetition of one of the options this week.

Reviewing the Week

Look back on the past week. What stands out to you the most as you have shifted from grieving the loss of Jesus to rejoicing in his astounding reappearance? Talk with God about it.

Contemplation of Jesus's Appearance to His Mother

Begin with a preparatory prayer to ready your heart for the following contemplation. Take some time to play each scene like a movie in your mind. Let your imagination bring you to these places. Afterward, close with the suggested prayer.

Scene 1: Picture the scenes prior to the resurrection. Jesus has died. After his physical death, he visits *Sheol* to preach to the imprisoned spirits (I Peter 3:19). Then he returns to the tomb to rise again. Jesus is about to see his mother, Mary.

Scene 2: Notice Mary's house, the rooms, the details. Mary is mourning. Imagine Jesus suddenly coming onto the scene. What might the encounter have been like? What would Mary have felt when seeing her dear son again after all that had transpired? What might Jesus have felt or done when seeing his mother?

Closing Prayer: Spirit of Life, fill me with gladness and joy to celebrate Jesus the Lord who is alive today and invites me into relationship and collaborative mission.

Week 31
Resurrection Stories, Part 2

Spirit of Life, fill me with gladness and joy to celebrate Jesus the Lord who is alive today and invites me into relationship and collaborative mission.

Option 1

Scripture: Luke 24:9–12

Reflection: Enter the scene. What words, phrases, or images stand out to you the most? What might God be showing you? How has resurrection affected you?

Option 2

Scripture: Luke 24:13–35

Reflection: Enter the scene with your senses. Where are you in the story? How does this encounter deepen your understanding of who Jesus is?

Option 3

Reflection: Spend some time contemplating the words to the song "Now the Green Blade Riseth" by John Macleod Campbell Crum (see links at "Supplements"). How has this been true in your own life? Talk with God about it. Close by singing it with a spirit of joy.

Option 4

Scripture: 1 Thessalonians 4:13–18

Reflection: Contemplate the hope of your own resurrection.

Option 5

Art Reflection: Jesus's post-resurrection appearance: "Supper at Emmaus" by Caravaggio. What stands out to you?

Option 6

Repetition of one of the options for this week.

Reviewing the Week

Look back on the past week. What stands out to you the most as you have prayed and reflected on encountering the Risen Christ? Talk with God about your reflections.

Week 32
Resurrection Stories, Part 3

Spirit of Life, fill me with gladness and joy to celebrate Jesus the Lord who is alive today and invites me into relationship and collaborative mission.

Option 1

Reflection: "What Did Jesus Do with His Resurrected Body?" (p. 162)

Option 2

Scripture: Matthew 28:16–20
Reflection: Enter the scene with all your senses. Notice the landscape, the people present. Where are you in the story?

Option 3

Reflection: Think back over the last week or so. Where have you seen resurrection? What life-giving stories have you read? What encounters have you had or observed that were life-infused? Make a list of all you recall and spend some time daydreaming about these. Then, make a conscious decision to look for signs of resurrection in the coming days as a spiritual practice.

Option 4

Scripture: I Corinthians 15:6–8; Acts 9:1–19

Reflection: Visualize these various encounters. Talk with God about them.

Option 5

Repetition of any of the days this week.

Option 6

Reflection: Contemplate the various appearances of Jesus you have looked at these past two weeks. What do you notice about the different ways the resurrected Jesus interacted with people? What kind of person is he?

Reviewing the Week

Look back on the past week. What stands out to you the most as you have prayed and reflected on encountering the Risen Christ? Talk with God about your reflections.

What Did Jesus Do with His Resurrected Body?

When I was growing up, Easter was all about vivid colors, hand-made dresses, savory food, baskets of candy, and family gatherings. The celebration started in church where we sang "He is alive!" like we meant it. Resurrection Day was a reminder of *life*. But missing from my memories is the story of Jesus *after* his initial reappearance. The narrative seemed to culminate and end with the empty tomb, and we all went back to school and work the next day.

Ignatius of Loyola saw beyond the empty tomb. He encouraged meditations on the life of Jesus after the stone had been rolled away. What did the glorified King of kings, Lord of lords, now enthroned Master of the Universe find fitting to do with his remaining time on earth before ascending? Ignatius recommended contemplation on these important scenes of Jesus's post-resurrection activity:

- Jesus's encounter with Mary Magdalene and his other women disciples (Mark 16:1–11; Matthew 28:8–10; Luke 23:55–24:12; John 20:11–18).
- Peter's race to the tomb seeking Jesus (Luke 24:9–12).
- Jesus's walk with the two disciples on their way to Emmaus (Luke 24:13–35; see also Mark 16:12–13).
- Jesus's visit with the disciples gathered in a house (John 20:19–23; Luke 24:36–48; Mark 16:14).
- Jesus's conversation with Thomas (John 20:24–29).
- Jesus's meal with his disciples who were fishing (John 21:1–23).
- Jesus's appearance to a crowd of five hundred (I Corinthians 15:6).
- Jesus's interaction with James (I Corinthians 15:7)
- Jesus's conversation with the disciples on Mt. Olive (Acts 1:1–2).
- Jesus's appearance to Saul, also named Paul (Acts 9:1–

19; I Corinthians 15:8; technically after the ascension but still included by Ignatius for contemplation).

Jesus hung around for forty days eating, walking, cooking, chatting, and teaching in his resurrected body. Ignatius suggested reading these scenes with all five senses to really enter the stories and understand them. In fact, he said as sensory creatures we can become the human beings we were created to be by imitating the fully human Jesus. Even in his glorified state, Jesus did not lose his humanity. He is the model of how to live the sensate life both before and after his resurrection. That is certainly true of one of my favorite post-resurrection stories: Jesus making a meal for his disciples on the beach. It is worth taking a few moments to reflect on part of this scene.

It was dawn, light just beginning to streak across the dark sky. Several of Jesus' disciples had been fishing all night. Water slapped rhythmically against the side of the boat as it rocked on the waves. The men were tired and wet. Their work had been in vain. No fish. The shore was not far, maybe 100 yards, but they didn't notice Jesus standing on the beach watching them. Then they heard a voice shouting advice across the water: "Throw your nets over on the right side. That is where all the fish are." The disciples did not recognize him. Perhaps they thought him a friendly stranger and figured what the heck. They had nothing to lose. They heaved their nets to the other side with little anticipation. But the lethargy quickly turned into excitement. The nets were filling up. Ridiculously, filling up! It was crazy! They couldn't even pull in the nets. That's when John exclaimed to Peter, "It's the Lord!"

After Jesus had called out his miraculous advice, he started a fire on the beach. He blew on the embers, stoking the flames. Fire crackled, warmth radiated, and the scent of smoke wafted upwards. Jesus sat and waited. He watched his friends wrestling with the now heavy nets of fish. He heard John shout his recognition, "It's the Lord!" He saw Peter throw off his work clothes and leap into the water, leaving the others to bring in the haul. No doubt Jesus felt delight, hearing and seeing their excitement as he anticipated eating breakfast with them.

Jesus knew how the scenario would play out. He had already started the fire with the intention of cooking for his tired friends. In fact, there was already fish and bread laid out when they walked up. Jesus asked for some of their catch to add to the flames. Then he said, "Come have breakfast." It was a welcome invitation after a long hard night of work. They sat down and Jesus served them, handing each a piece of bread and fish.

I wish I had been there. The feel of the pebbly sand under my feet, the crackling sound and scents of fire, the sight of the sun coming up over the lake in vibrant colors. And most of all the feeling of elation sitting with my best friend who only days before I believed was dead. Such an ordinary moment eating breakfast after work, yet amazingly wonderful. The simple made glorious by God's tangible presence.

As Howard Gray, SJ once pointed out, Jesus could have done all kinds of things with his resurrected self. He could have taken revenge on those who tortured and killed him. He could have demanded everyone bow down to him. He could have shown off the wonders of his new body. But instead he made himself a servant. Jesus watched with care from the shore even when his friends did not see or recognize him. He took on the menial task of cooking and serving a meal. He shared his time and presence. Jesus was the same person after his resurrection as before. Humble and compassionate. And he *is* the same person now.

That is what the resurrection means to me. Not just a moment or day of joy remembering the empty tomb and the life we have been given, but watching the way Jesus modeled *how to live that life.*

Week 33
The Holy Spirit's Presence and Gifts

*Spirit of Life, fill me with gladness and joy to celebrate Jesus the
Lord who is alive today and invites me into relationship
and collaborative mission.*

Option 1

Scripture: Acts 1:1–11

Reflection: What do you notice as you enter the scene? (see
also Mark 1:8; John 14:15–17, 25–26; Acts 19:1–7).

Option 2

Scripture: Acts 2:1–33

Reflection: Walk into this story with your senses. What do
you notice? What is God like as revealed in the Holy Spirit?

Option 3

Reflection: Where have you recently seen the Spirit of Christ
active today in concrete ways? In what ways do you long for
the Spirit to empower you in God's work?

Option 4

Scripture: 1 Corinthians 12:1–13ff (see also Romans 12:6–8)

Reflection: What spiritual gifts has God given you? How
does that relate to your created purpose? Have you considered

"eagerly desiring" and asking God for a particular spiritual gift (1 Cor 14:1)?

Option 5

Scripture: Ephesians 4:1–16

Reflection: Read this passage on spiritual gifts two or three times. What specific words or phrases stand out to you the most? Talk with God about it.

Option 6

Repetition of any of the days this week. Spend some time in joy and gratitude over God's good gifts.

Reviewing the Week

Look back on the past week. What stands out to you the most as you have prayed and reflected on the Holy Spirit's presence and gifts? Talk with God about your reflections. Close with "Come Down, O Love Divine" by Bianco of Siena (p. 167).

Come Down, O Love Divine
by Bianco of Siena [49]

Come down, O love divine, seek thou this soul of mine,
And visit it with thine own ardor glowing.
O Comforter, draw near, within my heart appear,
And kindle it, Thy holy flame bestowing.

O let it freely burn, til earthly passions turn
To dust and ashes in its heat consuming;
And let Thy glorious light shine ever on my sight,
And clothe me round, the while my path illuming.

Let holy charity mine outward vesture be,
And lowliness become mine inner clothing;
True lowliness of heart, which takes the humbler part,
And o'er its own shortcomings weeps with loathing.

And so the yearning strong, with which the soul will long,
Shall far outpass the power of human telling;
For none can guess its grace, till he become the place
Wherein the Holy Spirit makes a dwelling.

---

[49] Bianco of Siena wrote the poem in the 14th century. It was translated to English, from Italian, by Richard F. Littledale in *The People's Hymnal* (London: Joseph Masters, 1867).

Week 34
Contemplation to Attain Love

Lord, I ask for a deep knowledge of all that I have received from you so that gratitude might inspire me to love and serve you in everything.

This week is a bit different. Instead of choosing an option, take time for *each* day's reflection. As you do, notice gifts you received from God during each segment of the Exercises.

Day 1

Reflection: Ignatius says love ought to find its expression primarily in deeds more than words. How has God acted in your life over the years? Write these specific things down and spend some time in gratitude.

Song: "My Redeemer is Faithful and True" by Steven Curtis Chapman or another worship song that reminds you of God's faithfulness to you.

Day 2

Reflection: Consider what surfaced for you while contemplating creation and God's love during the Principle and Foundation and the First Week. Keep in mind you are not doing a review of whole sections, but rather recalling what stands out to you the most. As you do this follow Ignatius' instruction (*SE* 234):

Bring to memory the benefits received, of creation, redemption, and particular gifts, pondering with much feeling how much God our Lord has done for me, and how much He has given me of what He has, and that the same Lord desires to give me himself as much as he can, according to his divine ordination. And with this to reflect on myself, considering with much reason and justice, what I ought on my side to offer and give to his Divine Majesty, that is to say, everything that is mine, and myself with it, as one who makes an offering with much feeling.

Day 3

Reflection: Consider what has surfaced for you when contemplating Jesus's ministry and sacrifice in the Second Week and Third Week. Keep in mind you are not doing a review of whole sections, but rather recalling what stood out to you the most. Then ponder these per Ignatius's instructions for Day 2.

Day 4

Reflection: Consider what has surfaced for you when contemplating Life and God-given gifts in the Fourth Week. Keep in mind you are not doing a review of the whole section, but rather recalling what stood out to you the most. Then ponder these per Ignatius's instructions in Day 2.

Day 5

Repetition of any of the days this week.

Day 6

Spend your day in praise and gratitude to God. Let your gratitude of God's love for you fuel your desire to give to others.

Reviewing the Week

Look back on the past week. What stands out to you the most as you have prayed and reflected on gratitude for God's gifts? Talk with God about it. Close with poem "Fall in Love" (p. 171).

Fall in Love
by Pedro Arrupe[50]

Nothing is more practical than
finding God, than
falling in love
in a quite absolute, final way.
What you are in love with,
what seizes your imagination, will affect everything.
It will decide
what will get you out of bed in the morning,
what you do with your evenings,
how you spend your weekends,
what you read, whom you know,
what breaks your heart,
and what amazes you with joy and gratitude.
Fall in love, stay in love,
and it will decide everything.

---

[50] Attributed to Jesuit Pedro Arrupe (1907–1991), but origin is
uncertain (he never published it). It has been popularly circulated for
many years, possibly written down by someone who heard him
speak.

Week 35
Contemplation to Attain Love, Part 2

Lord, I ask for a deep knowledge of all that I have received from you so that gratitude might inspire me to love and serve you in everything.

Option 1

Scripture: Acts 17:24–28

Reflection: Spend some time in wonder and awe at how God sustains all life and how in God we live and move and have our being. Contemplate how God dwells in you and that you are in union with God.

Option 2

Scripture: James 1:17; 1 John 4:10–11

Reflection: Contemplate with gratitude how God is the source of all good things, such as justice, goodness, empathy, love, and mercy. Think of concrete examples. In what specific ways might you pass on the good that God has given you?

Option 3

Reflection: Think back on the past day. Where have you noticed God's goodness? What do you feel thankful for?

Option 4

Scripture: Romans 12

Reflection: How can becoming aware of God's generosity inspire you to give as well? In what practical ways might you serve others in your daily life? Be specific.

Option 5

Repetition of a previous day this week.

Option 6

Ignatius's Prayer: "Take, Lord, and receive all my liberty, my memory, my intellect, and all my will—all that I have and possess. You gave it to me: to you, Lord, I return it! All is yours, dispose of it according to all your will. Give me your love and grace, for this is enough for me" (*SE* 234).

Reflection: Offer this prayer to God and spend time meditating on what this means specifically for you in daily life.

Reviewing the Week

Look back on the past week. What stands out to you the most as you have prayed and reflected on gratitude of God's gifts? Talk with God about your reflections. Close with "Take My Life and Let It Be" as your prayer (p. 174).

Take My Life and Let It Be
by Frances R. Havergal[51]

Take my life and let it be
consecrated, Lord, to Thee.
Take my moments and my days;
let them flow in endless praise.

Take my hands and let them move
at the impulse of Thy love.
Take my feet and let them be
swift and beautiful for Thee.

Take my voice and let me sing
always, only, for my King.
Take my lips and let them be
filled with messages from Thee.

Take my silver and my gold.
Not a mite would I withhold.
Take my intellect and use
every power as Thou dost choose.

Take my will and make it Thine.
It shall be no longer mine.
Take my heart it is Thine own.
It shall be thy royal throne.

Take my love; my Lord, I pour
at Thy feet its treasure store.
Take myself, and I will be
ever, only, all for Thee.

---

[51] First published in Charles Snepp, ed. *Appendix to Songs of Grace and Glory* (London: James Nisbet, 1874), 39–40.

Week 36
Reviewing the Journey

You have now completed all Four Weeks of the Spiritual Exercises! During these last several months you have covered the following:

From Principle and Foundation:
- Your image of God
- God's love for you
- Your relationship with other human beings and all creation
- Inner freedom
- Discernment of spiritual influences that pull us away or toward God (consolation and desolation)
- Emotions and the spiritual life
- The Examen

From First Week:
- Cosmic, global, and historical dimensions of sin
- Personal sin
- God's mercy
- Inner freedom and discernment (continued)
- Longing and praying for transformation (global and personal)

You have also been introduced to different types of prayer:

- Examen (continued)
- Praying with the body
- Traditional prayers (e.g. *Anima Christi*)
- Preparatory prayer
- Praying Scripture with the senses
- Triple Colloquies

From Second Week:

- Imagination and the spiritual life
- Anticipating the Kingdom
- Getting to know and admire Jesus
- Two Standards (to whose authority will you submit?)
- Discerning the spirits
- Humility and simplicity
- Inner freedom (continued)
- Making decisions

You have also been introduced to these practices:

- Reading Scripture with the senses
- Reflecting on art for the soul
- Imaginative contemplations/meditations
  - Contemplation of a Heroic Leader
  - Meditation on the Two Standards
  - Incarnation Contemplation
  - Three Types of People Meditation
  - Three Kinds of Humility

From the Third Week:

- Sorrow and compassion for Jesus's suffering
- Spiritual practice of empathizing with others
- Coming to terms with one's own suffering and death
- Greater willingness to suffer hardship for the sake of advancing God's good work.

Also, during the Third Week:
- Imaginative contemplation
  -Bethany to Jerusalem Contemplation

From the Fourth Week:
- Joyful celebration of life
- Getting to know and experience Jesus post-resurrection
- God's good gifts to us
- Spiritual gifts
- Loving union with God
- Grateful service to others

Also, this week:
- Imaginative contemplation
  -Contemplation of Jesus's Appearance to His Mother

This week, take some time to reflect on your experience of the Fourth Week, as well as the Spiritual Exercises as a whole. Look back over your journal and other sign posts. Ask God to bring to the surface what is most important for your spiritual process. As you reflect, keep prayer at the center (not just an intellectual or meditative review). The goal is always connection with God.

Reflections on the Fourth Week
- What emotions and desires arise as you reflect on your experience of the Fourth Week?
- What stands out to you the most? (e.g. Recurring patterns? Specific images or Scriptures?)
- In what ways has your imagination been shaped during the Fourth Week?
- What is something you have discovered about who God is from your encounter with the Holy Spirit?
- What practical ways have you decided to return God's love and gifts by serving others?

Reflections on the Spiritual Exercises

- What has this experience of going through the Exercises been like for you? What stands out to you the most?
- What has prayer been like for you during these last several months? What have you heard from God?
- What is your image of the Triune God at the end of the Exercises compared to the beginning? What is your image of the Father, Jesus, and the Holy Spirit?
- How are things going with practicing spiritual discernment and decision-making?
- What concrete actions is God inviting you to take?
- Are there particular areas you want to spend more time on? Any places where you are struggling?
- What do you hope for as you conclude the Exercises and incorporate your experience going forward?
- Are there others you know who might benefit from going through the Spiritual Exercises as well?

Ignatius of Loyola hoped that by the end of the retreat you would know God's love deeply and return God's love in such a way as to be love to others. The Exercises are not only for personal enrichment; they are especially about shaping the way you move in the world. They are about imbibing and imitating Jesus so as to use your gifts to help others. This is why discernment and decision-making are so integral to the Exercises—active love involves making concrete choices on a daily basis. Do you feel your experience with the Spiritual Exercises has achieved its purpose? Talk with your spiritual director about your reflections and practical next steps.

Love is a daily commitment and process—not something we someday "arrived at" and no longer need to nurture. The journey continues beyond the Spiritual Exercise.

Close with prayer, including the two on the following page.

Closing Prayers:

O God, may my love for you ever increase and may I know how wide and deep is your love for me. Guide me in the next steps as I finish the Exercises and continue to seek you and your purposes. Empower me by your Spirit to love and serve others on a daily basis in concrete and specific ways. Amen.

"Take, Lord, and receive
all my liberty, my memory, my intellect, and all my will—
all that I have and possess.
You gave it to me: to you, Lord, I return it!
All is yours, dispose of it according to all your will.
Give me your love and grace,
for this is enough for me" (*SE* 234)

ABOUT THE AUTHOR

Karen R. Keen is a spiritual director, educator, and author. She became fascinated by the Spiritual Exercises while completing the Training Program for the Ministry of Spiritual Direction under the auspices of the Faithful Companions of Jesus (FCJ), a congregation of Catholic sisters in the Ignatian tradition. She has received training in the Spiritual Exercises from Howard Gray, SJ, and Michael Dante, director of the Faber Center for Ignatian Spirituality at Marquette University. Karen has a background in counseling (MS, Western Oregon University), as well as biblical and theological studies (MA, Western Seminary; ThM, Duke Divinity School). She can be contacted through her ministry, The Redwood Center for Spiritual Care and Education at redwoodspiritualcare.com.

Made in the USA
Las Vegas, NV
19 December 2022

63430830R10111